U.S. DEPARTMENT OF TRANSPORTATION

FEDERAL AVIATION ADMINISTRATION

WILDLIFE STRIKES TO CIVIL AIRCRAFT IN THE UNITED STATES 1990–2012

U.S. DEPARTMENT OF AGRICULTURE

ANIMAL AND PLANT HEALTH INSPECTION SERVICE

WILDLIFE SERVICES

FEDERAL AVIATION ADMINISTRATION
NATIONAL WILDLIFE STRIKE DATABASE
SERIAL REPORT NUMBER 19

REPORT OF THE ASSOCIATE ADMINISTRATOR OF AIRPORTS
OFFICE OF AIRPORT SAFETY AND STANDARDS
AIRPORT SAFETY & CERTIFICATION
WASHINGTON, DC

SEPTEMBER 2013

The Federal Aviation Administration produced this report in cooperation with the U. S. Department of Agriculture, Animal and Plant Health Inspection Service (APHIS), Wildlife Services.

AUTHORS

Richard A. Dolbeer, Science Advisor, Airport Wildlife Hazards Program, U.S. Department of Agriculture, APHIS, Wildlife Services, 6100 Columbus Ave., Sandusky, OH 44870

Sandra E. Wright, Wildlife Strike Database Manager, Airport Wildlife Hazards Program, U.S. Department of Agriculture, APHIS, Wildlife Services, 6100 Columbus Ave., Sandusky, OH 44870

John Weller, National Wildlife Biologist, Office of Airport Safety and Standards, Federal Aviation Administration, 800 Independence Ave., SE, Washington, DC 20591

Michael J. Begier, National Coordinator, Airport Wildlife Hazards Program, U.S. Department of Agriculture, APHIS, Wildlife Services, 1400 Independence Ave., SW, Washington, DC 20250

COVER PHOTOGRAPH

A B-757-200 flew through a flock of about 20 double-crested cormorants (mean body mass = 5.2 lbs) at 800 feet on climb from an east coast airport in April 2012, causing extensive damage to the #2 engine. The flight crew declared an emergency and returned safely to the airport. Photo courtesy of airport.

The double-crested cormorant population in North America has increased at an average annual rate of 6.1 percent from 1980 to 2011. Data from the North American Breeding Bird Survey (BBS).

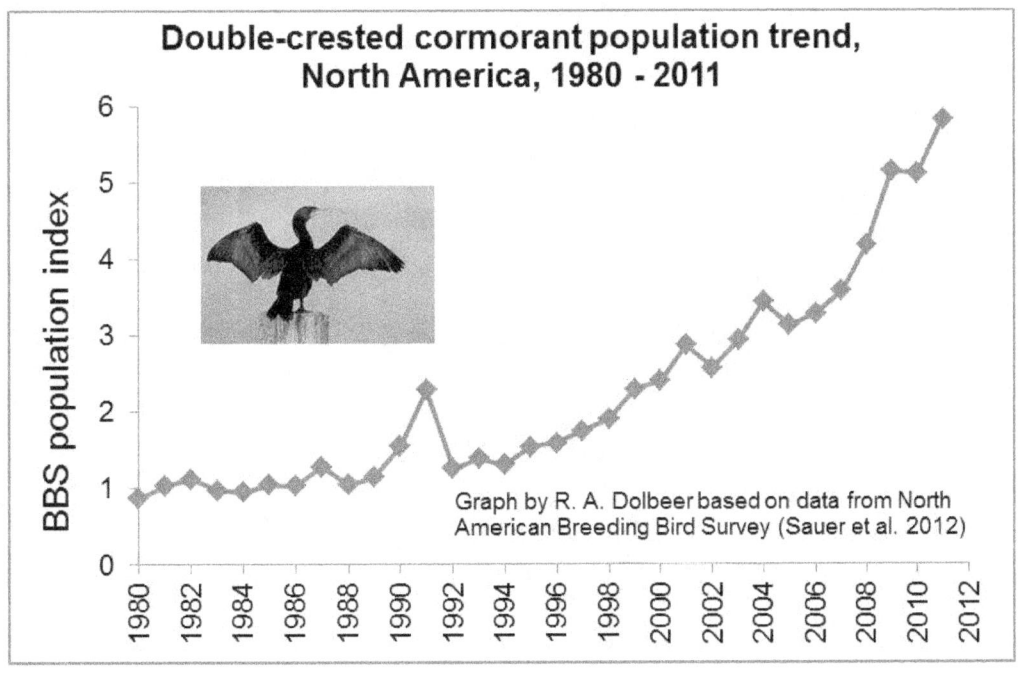

Double-crested cormorant population trend, North America, 1980 - 2011

Graph by R. A. Dolbeer based on data from North American Breeding Bird Survey (Sauer et al. 2012)

TABLE OF CONTENTS

LIST OF TABLES

LIST OF FIGURES

LIST OF APPENDICES

ACKNOWLEDGMENTS

We acknowledge and thank all of the people who took the time and effort to report wildlife strikes— pilots, mechanics, control tower personnel, airport operations personnel, airline flight safety officers, airport wildlife biologists, and many others. Sponsorship and funds for the ongoing maintenance and analysis of the FAA Wildlife Strike Database are provided by the FAA, Office of Airport Safety and Standards, Washington, DC, and the Airports Research and Development Branch, FAA William J. Hughes Technical Center, Atlantic City, NJ. We thank Roger Nicholson, Boeing Aircraft Company, for timely advice during the development of this report.

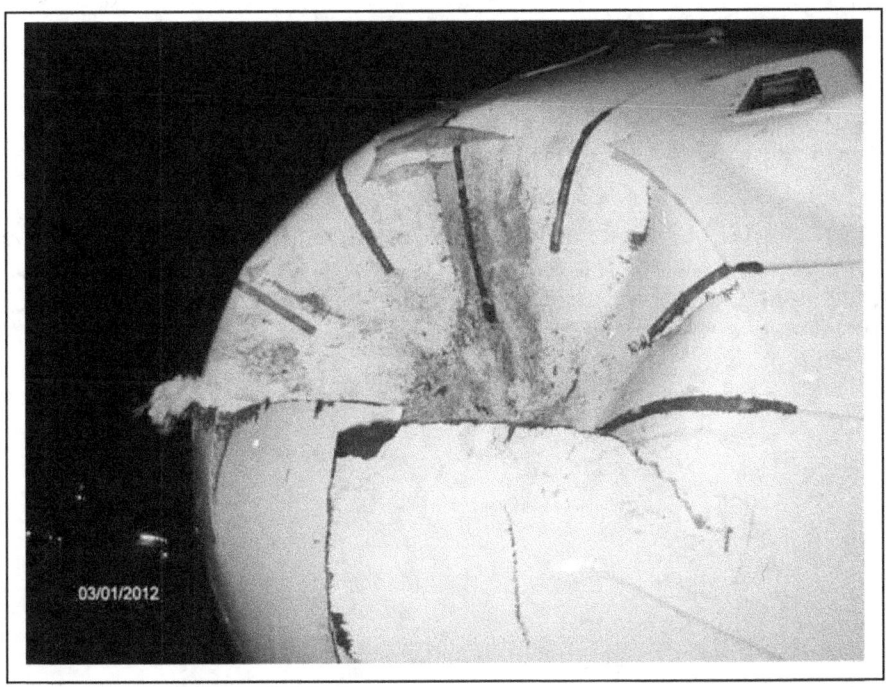

An MD-11 flew through a flock of migrating snow geese at night at 8,500 feet on climb from a southern airport, Mar 2012, causing damage to the radome, 1 engine, wing, and fuselage. The flight crew declared an emergency and returned safely to the airport. At least 11 impact points were identified on the aircraft. Repair costs exceeded $2 million. Photo courtesy of aircraft operator.

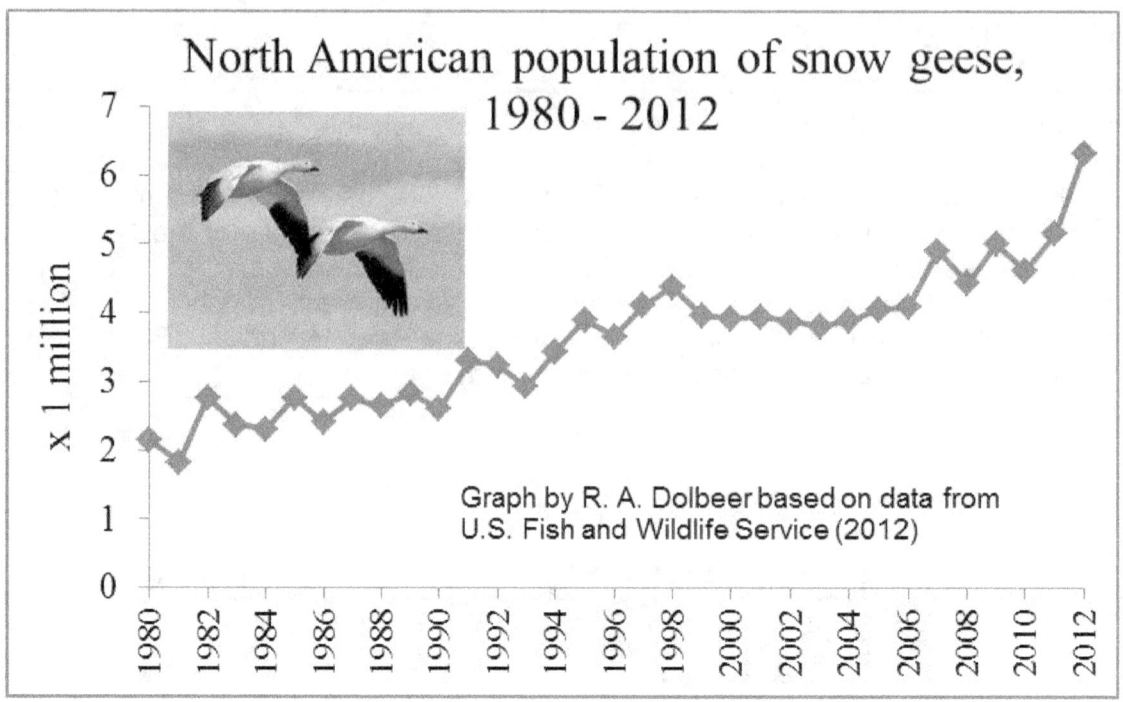

From 1990 to 2012, 109 strikes involving snow geese and civil aircraft were reported in the USA; 58 percent of these incidents involved multiple birds struck. Snow geese are primarily a threat to aircraft during climb and approach phases of flight outside airport boundaries; 90 percent of the strikes occurred at $\geq$500 feet AGL and 68% occurred at $\geq$1,500 feet AGL.

EXECUTIVE SUMMARY – FAA WILDLIFE MITIGATION

In 2012, the FAA and USDA continued to make great progress with its multifaceted approach for mitigating wildlife strikes. The FAA ensured that 100 percent of Part 139 airports have completed a Wildlife Hazard Assessment (WHA), are in the process of conducting a WHA, or have taken a Federal grant to conduct a WHA. Strike reporting continued to increase, especially with General Aviation (GA) aircraft, which increased strike reporting by 11 percent between 2011 and 2012. The FAA implemented three performance metrics to monitor strike reporting trends and GA wildlife mitigation. The performance metrics include percentage of damaging strikes, strike reporting rates, and tracking of General Aviation (GA) airports that conduct WHAs and site visits. We also issued a final Advisory Circular (AC) on strike reporting and draft ACs on WHA methodology and requirements for federally obligated public airports to conduct WHAs. We have expanded outreach to increase general aviation strike reporting, continued a robust research program, and incorporated new technology to allow simplified and paperless strike reporting. The FAA also continued to provide Airport Improvement Program (AIP) funding to airports to conduct WHAs and develop Wildlife Hazard Management Plans (WHMPs). These efforts have led to increased strike reporting in both commercial and general aviation. While strike reporting has increased, significant, damaging strikes have remained stable.

The FAA continued to distribute the latest Report Wildlife Strikes awareness poster throughout 2012. Overall, 24,000 posters have been distributed to more than 4,000 Part 139 airports, GA airports, aviation flight schools and the aviation industry in the last two years. The distribution of strike awareness posters is one of several outreach activities to improve strike reporting and safety at airports.

The FAA continues work with industry to encourage all certificated airports to conduct WHAs, even if the certificated airport has not experienced one of the triggering events specified in Part 139. To date, 100 percent of Part 139 airports have completed a WHA, are in the process of conducting a WHA, or have taken a Federal grant to conduct a WHA. The FAA also encourages federally obligated GA airports to conduct WHAs or Wildlife Hazard Site Visits (WHSV) to provide fundamental wildlife and habitat information for an effective, airport-specific, wildlife hazard mitigation program.

Our research efforts continue. The cooperative FAA/USDA APHIS WS National Wildlife Research Center (NWRC) continues its efforts to improve wildlife management techniques and practices on and near airports. These efforts include:
- Alternatives to habitat management to reduce attraction to hazardous species
- Techniques for controlling species by restricting access to attractive features like storm water ponds
- Technologies for harassing and deterring hazardous species
- Evaluation of avian radar systems for detecting and tracking birds on or near airports
- Aircraft-mounted alternating, pulse lights to enhance aircraft detection and deter wildlife strikes

The FAA continues to evaluate the capability of commercially available, low-cost, portable radars to reliably detect and track birds on or near airports. The Center of Excellence for Airport Technology (CEAT) at the University of Illinois has served as the FAA's research partner for the performance assessments of bird radar. The initial avian radar systems have involved Accipiter Radar Technologies Inc. and were deployed at Seattle-Tacoma and Whidbey Island Naval Station in 2007, Chicago O'Hare in 2009, and John F. Kennedy and Dallas-Fort Worth in 2010.

Additional evaluations have continued through FAA's multi-year agreement with USDA who teamed up with the National Center of Atmospheric Research (NCAR) and Indiana State University to further evaluate the performance of bird radar systems. The effort brings together experts in wildlife biology, ornithology, radar engineering, and system integration from government, industry, and academia to evaluate the MERLIN Avian Radar System by DeTect, Inc., one of several radar systems used to detect birds at and near airports. The assessment effort is part of the FAA's overall investigation into the effectiveness of commercially available avian radar detection systems at U.S. civil airports when used in conjunction with other known wildlife management and control techniques. Though it is well established that radar can detect wild birds, there is little published information concerning the accuracy and detection capabilities related to range, altitude, target size, and effects of weather for avian radar systems.

In November, 2010, the FAA published a performance specification in the form of an Advisory Circular 150/5220-25, *Airport Avian Radar Systems*, which airports can use to competitively purchase bird radar systems. The guidelines provide the operational considerations of acquiring and using the technology to enhance wildlife hazard mitigation practices on civil airports. Under some circumstances, procurement of bird radar systems may be eligible for funding under the FAA's Airport Improvement Program. A new research effort began at the end of 2011 and continued through 2012 that will examine the feasibility and practicality of pilots and air traffic controllers using bird radar data.

The FAA funded and assisted with the development of two new Airport Cooperative Research Program (ACRP) reports to aid General Aviation airports with the mitigation of wildlife hazards. Two-thousand seven hundred and seventy copies of ACRP Report 32, *Guidebook for Addressing Aircraft/ Wildlife Hazards at General Aviation Airports,* and ACRP Synthesis 23, *Bird Harassment, Repellent, and Deterrent Techniques for Use on and Near Airports,* were distributed in October 2011 and early 2012 to all federally obligated National Plan of Integrated Airport System (NPIAS) General Aviation airports. The reports, published in 2010 and 2011 respectively, provide practical guidance and specific techniques on how to address wildlife strikes at airports with a specific emphasis on the general aviation community.

In 2010 and continuing through 2012, the FAA, USDA, Airlines for America (i.e., formerly the Air Transport Association) and the Air Line Pilots Association developed review methodologies to better understand the wildlife strike/ aviation problem in concert with the Joint Implementation Measurement and Data Analysis Team (JIMDAT).

The Commercial Aviation Safety Team (CAST) determined that JIMDAT would track wildlife strikes and provide periodic monitoring reports to CAST concerning wildlife strikes. During a February 2013 CAST meeting, CAST fully approved JIMDAT "Option 2" Birdstrike monitoring proposal. This included reporting fatality risk values at appropriate intervals and trending egregious events to provide confidence.

Technological advances have helped ease and streamline the strike reporting process. The form used to report wildlife strikes, FAA Form 5200-7, *Bird/Other Wildlife Strike Report,* has been available online since April 2001. In addition, the FAA developed mobile application software that allows strike reporting from your smart phone. An extension to the mobile application software also placed a Quick Response (QR) Code for smart phones on the bottom of the 2011– 2012 "Report Wildlife Strikes" poster, which allows anyone to report a wildlife strike via the web or their personal data devices. As a result, electronic filings have dramatically increased every year after. Last year, 86 percent of the 10,726 strike reports were filed electronically.

EXECUTIVE SUMMARY – STRIKE DATA

Increased media attention to wildlife strikes with aircraft, such as the emergency forced landing of US Airways Flight 1549 in the Hudson River on 15 January 2009 after Canada geese were ingested in both engines on the Airbus 320, has dramatically demonstrated to the public that wildlife strikes are a serious but manageable aviation safety issue. However, the civil and military aviation communities have long recognized that the threat from aircraft collisions with wildlife is real and increasing. Globally, wildlife strikes have killed more than 250 people and destroyed over 229 aircraft since 1988. Factors that contribute to this increasing threat are increasing populations of large birds and increasing air traffic by quieter, turbofan-powered aircraft.

This report presents a summary analysis of data from the National Wildlife Strike Database for the 23-year period 1990 through 2012. A sample of significant wildlife strikes to civil aircraft in the USA during 2012 is also included as an appendix.

The number of strikes annually reported has increased 5.8-fold from 1,851 in 1990 to a record 10,726 in 2012 (131,096 strikes for 1990–2012). The rate of annual increase has averaged 4 percent over the last four years since the pronounced rise following the US Airways Flight 1549 incident; the increase from 2011 to 2012 was 6 percent. Between 2011 and 2012, GA aircraft strike reports increased at almost twice the rate (11 percent) than the remainder of civil aircraft strike reporting. Birds were involved in 97.0 percent of the reported strikes, terrestrial mammals in 2.2 percent, bats in 0.6 percent and reptiles in 0.1 percent (Table 1). Although the number of reported strikes has steadily increased, the number of reported damaging strikes has actually declined from 764 in 2000 to 606 in 2012. The decline in damaging strikes has been most pronounced for commercial aircraft in the airport environment (at ≤500 feet above ground level [AGL]).

Damaging strikes have not declined for General Aviation aircraft or for commercial aircraft above 500 feet AGL.

In 2012, 86 percent and 4 percent of the 10,726 strike reports were filed using the electronic and paper versions, respectively, of FAA Form 5200-7, Bird/Other Wildlife Strike Report. Since the online version of this form became available in April 2001, use of the electronic reporting system has climbed dramatically.

The number of USA airports with strikes reported increased from 332 in 1990 to a record 643 in 2012. The 643 airports with strikes reported in 2012 were comprised of 387 airports certificated for passenger service under 14 CFR Part 139 and 256 general aviation airports. From 1990 - 2012, strikes have been reported from 1,771 USA airports.

Fifty-two percent of bird strikes occurred between July and October; 30 percent of deer strikes occurred in October–November. Terrestrial mammals are more likely to be struck at night (63 percent) whereas birds are struck more often during the day (62 percent). Both birds (60 percent) and terrestrial mammals (64 percent) are more likely to be struck during the landing (i.e., descent, approach or landing roll) phase of flight compared to take-off and climb (37 percent and 34 percent, respectively).

For commercial and GA aircraft, 72 and 74 percent of bird strikes, respectively, occurred at or below 500 feet AGL. Above 500 feet AGL, the number of strikes declined by 34 percent for each 1,000-foot gain in height for commercial aircraft, and by 42 percent for GA aircraft. Strikes occurring above 500 feet were more likely to cause damage than strikes at or below 500 feet. The record height for a reported bird strike was 31,300 feet.

From 1990 to 2012, 482 species of birds, 42 species of terrestrial mammals, 15 species of bats, and 11 species of reptiles were identified as struck by aircraft. Waterfowl, gulls, and raptors are the species groups of birds with the most damaging strikes; Artiodactyls (mainly deer) and carnivores (mainly coyotes) are the terrestrial mammals with the most damaging strikes. Although the percentage of bird strikes with reported damage has averaged 9 percent for the 23-year period, this number has declined from 18 percent in 1990 to 6 percent in 2012. For terrestrial mammals (23-year average of 34 percent), the decline has been from 83 percent in 1990 to 16 percent in 2012.

Also noted from 1990–2012, a negative effect-on-flight was reported in 7 percent and 23 percent of the bird and terrestrial mammal strike reports, respectively. Precautionary/emergency landing after striking wildlife was the most commonly reported negative effect (4,538 incidents), including 45 incidents in which the pilot jettisoned fuel (an average of 13,280 gallons) to lighten aircraft weight and 80 incidents in which an overweight landing was made. Aborted takeoff was the second most commonly reported negative effect (1,990 incidents). These negative incidents included 836 aborted takeoffs at ≥80 knots.

The hazard level for 86 bird species with 50 or more strikes, based on a composite of the percent of strikes causing damage, major damage, and a negative effect-on-flight, ranged from 1 percent or less for 30 species to 53 percent for snow geese.

Sixty strikes have resulted in a destroyed aircraft; forty (60 percent) of these occurred at general aviation airports. The annual cost of wildlife strikes to the USA civil aviation industry is projected to be 583,175 hours of aircraft downtime and $957 million in direct and other monetary losses.

This analysis of 23 years of strike data documents the progress being made in reducing damaging strikes at Part 139 certificated airports. Management actions to mitigate the risk have been implemented at many airports since the 1990s; these efforts are likely responsible for the general decline in reported strikes with damage from 2000–2012 in spite of continued increases in populations of many large bird species. However, much work remains to be done to reduce wildlife strikes. Management actions at airports should be prioritized based on the hazard level of species (Table 19) observed in the aircraft operating area.

The successful mitigation efforts at airports that have reduced damaging strikes in recent years have done little to reduce strikes outside the airport boundaries. To address strikes above 500 feet AGL, the general public and aviation community must first widen its view of wildlife management to minimize hazardous wildlife attractants within 5 miles of airports. Second, on-going research and mitigation efforts to further develop and incorporate avian radar and bird migration forecasting and to study avian sensory perception to enhance aircraft detection and avoidance by birds should be maintained. Third, Federal guidance on wildlife hazards at airports should continue to be reviewed, and where necessary revised, to incorporate new information about wildlife hazards and wildlife strike reporting trends. Finally, Part 139 certificated airports, general aviation facilities, aircraft operators and the aviation industry should continue to provide as much detailed information as possible about wildlife strikes, such as species identification and number of wildlife struck, time and altitude of strike, and damage costs.

This annual report is based on information from a portion of the available data fields contained in the National Wildlife Strike Database. These reports provide summary information on the nature of wildlife strikes in a format that continues to be found useful by the aviation industry. The database is available to the public. Interested parties can query and examine the data independently at the FAA wildlife strike database website (http://wildlife.faa.gov). The web site has search fields that enable users to find data on specific airports, airlines, aircraft, and engine types, as well as damage incurred, date of strike, species struck, and state without having to download the entire database. The FAA has also developed software to make strike reporting easier. Now, anyone who needs to report a wildlife strike can do so via the web or mobile devices like the Blackberry and iPhone.

This page intentionally left blank

WILDLIFE STRIKES TO CIVIL AIRCRAFT IN THE UNITED STATES, 1990–2012

A Cessna Citation II operated by the Department of Homeland Security hit a white-tailed deer during landing roll at an airport in South Carolina, 17 Nov 2012. The collision ruptured a fuel tank; the ensuing fire destroyed the aircraft. The flight crew escaped unharmed. From 1990–2012, 1,037 deer were struck by civil aircraft in USA; 18% of these strikes occurred in November (see Figure 6).

INTRODUCTION

The emergency forced landing of US Airways Flight 1549 in the Hudson River on 15 January 2009 after Canada geese were ingested in both engines on the Airbus 320 (National Transportation Safety Board 2010, Marra et al. 2009) dramatically demonstrated to the public at large that bird strikes are a serious aviation safety issue. However, the civil and military aviation communities have long recognized that the threat to human health and safety from aircraft collisions with wildlife (wildlife strikes) is real and increasing (Dolbeer 2000, MacKinnon et al. 2001). Globally, wildlife strikes have killed more than 250 people and destroyed over 229 aircraft since 1988 including the 19-fatality crash of a Dornier 228-200 in Nepal in September 2012 after a vulture was struck on take-off (Richardson and West 2000; Thorpe 2003; 2005; 2012, Dolbeer, unpublished data).

Three factors contribute to this increasing threat:

1. Many populations of large bird and mammal species commonly involved in strikes have increased markedly in the last few decades and adapted to living in urban environments, including airports. For example, the resident (non-migratory) Canada goose population in the USA and Canada increased from about 0.5 million to 3.8 million from 1980 to 2012 (Dolbeer et al. 2013). During the same time period, the North American snow goose population increased from about 2 million to 6 million birds (U.S. Fish and Wildlife Service. 2012). Other large-bird species that have shown significant population

All 19 passengers and crew died when a Nepalese-based Dornier 228-200 struck a vulture and crashed shortly after take-off in Kathmandu, Sep 2012.

increases from 1980 to 2011 include bald eagles (6.2 percent annual rate of increase), wild turkeys (9.5 percent), turkey vultures (2.6 percent), American white pelicans (8.5 percent), double-crested cormorants (6.1 percent), sandhill cranes (6.1 percent), great blue herons (1.3 percent), and red-tailed hawks (1.8 percent, Sauer et al. 2012). Thirteen of the 14 bird species in North America with mean body masses greater than 8 pounds (3.6 kilograms) showed significant population increases from 1970 to the early 1990s (Dolbeer and Eschenfelder 2003). The white-tailed deer population increased from a low of about 350,000 in 1900 to about 15 million in 1984 and to over 28 million by 2010 (McCabe and McCabe 1997, VerCauteren et al. 2011).

2. Concurrent with population increases of many large bird species, air traffic has increased since 1980. Passenger enplanements in the USA increased from about 310 million in 1980 to 725 million in 2012 (2.7 percent per year), and commercial air traffic increased from about 18 million aircraft movements in 1980 to 23 million in 1990. From 1991 to 2013, commercial air traffic has fluctuated between 24 million and 29 million movements per year, Table 2, Federal Aviation Administration 2013a). Commercial air traffic in the USA is predicted to grow at a rate of about 1.4 percent per year from 25 million movements in 2012 to 32 million by 2030.

3. Commercial air carriers have replaced their older three or four-engine aircraft fleets with more efficient and quieter, two-engine aircraft. In 1965, about 87 percent of the 1,037 turbine-powered passenger aircraft in the USA had three or four engines. By 1990, the fleet had grown to 5,743 turbine-powered aircraft of which 32 percent had 3 or 4 engines. In 2008, only 8 percent of the 7,371 turbine-powered aircraft had three or four engines (U.S. Department of Transportation 2013). With the steady advances in technology over the past several decades, today's two-engine aircraft are more powerful than yesterday's three and four-engine aircraft, and they are more reliable. However, in the event of a multiple ingestion event (e.g., the US Airways

Flight 1549 incident on 15 January 2009), aircraft with two engines may have vulnerabilities not shared by their three or four engine-equipped counterparts. In addition, previous research has indicated that birds are less able to detect and avoid modern jet aircraft with quieter turbofan engines (Chapter 3, International Civil Aviation Organization 1993) than older aircraft with noisier (Chapter 2) engines (Burger 1983, Kelly et al. 1999).

As a result of these factors, experts within the Federal Aviation Administration (FAA), U.S. Department of Agriculture (USDA), U.S. Navy and U.S. Air Force expect the risk of wildlife-aircraft collisions to be a continuing challenge over the next decade.

The FAA has initiated several programs to address this important safety issue. Among the various programs is the collection and analysis of data from wildlife strikes. The FAA began collecting wildlife strike data in 1965. However, except for cursory examinations of the strike reports to determine general trends, the data were never submitted to rigorous analysis until the 1990s. In 1995, the FAA, through an interagency agreement with the USDA, Wildlife Services, (USDA/WS), initiated a project to obtain more objective estimates of the magnitude and nature of the national wildlife strike problem for civil aviation. This project involves having specialists from the USDA/WS: (1) edit all strike reports (FAA Form 5200-7, *Bird/Other Wildlife Strike Report*) received by the FAA since 1990 to ensure consistent, error-free data; (2) enter all edited strike reports in the FAA National Wildlife Strike Database; (3) supplement FAA-reported strikes with additional, non-duplicated strike reports from other sources; (4) provide the FAA with an updated computer file each month containing all edited strike reports; and (5) assist the FAA with the production of annual and special reports summarizing the results of analyses of the data from the National Wildlife Strike Database. Such analyses are critical to determining the economic cost of wildlife strikes, the magnitude of safety issues, and most important, the nature of the problems (e.g., wildlife species involved, types of damage, height and phase of flight during which strikes occur, and seasonal patterns). The information obtained from these analyses provides the foundation for FAA national policies and guidance and for refinements in the development and implementation of integrated research and management efforts to reduce wildlife strikes. Data on the number of strikes causing damage to

The bald eagle nesting population in the contiguous USA has increased from about 1,000 pairs to over 14,000 pairs, 1980–2012. This radio-tagged juvenile eagle was released after removal from a Midwestern airport to help biologists track movements and devise plans to keep the birds separated from aircraft. Nine bald eagles were struck in 8 strike events with civil aircraft in 2012. Photo, USDA.

aircraft or other adverse effects (e.g., aborted take-off) also provide a benchmark for individual airports to evaluate and improve their Wildlife Hazard Management Plans in the context of a Safety Management System (Dolbeer and Begier 2012).

The first annual report on wildlife strikes to civil aircraft in the USA was completed in November 1995 (Dolbeer et al. 1995). This is the 19th report in the series and covers the 23-year period, 1990–2012. Current and historic annual reports are accessible as PDF files at http://www.faa.gov/airports/airport_safety/wildlife/.

To supplement the statistical summary of data presented in tables and graphs, a sample of significant wildlife strikes to civil aircraft in the USA during 2012 is presented in Appendix A. These recent strike examples demonstrate the widespread and diverse nature of the problem. A more extensive list of significant strike events, 1990–2012, is available at http://www.faa.gov/airports/airport_safety/wildlife/.

RESULTS

NUMBER OF REPORTED STRIKES AND STRIKES WITH DAMAGE

The number of strikes annually reported to the FAA has increased 5.8-fold from 1,851 in 1990 to a record 10,726 in 2012 (Table 1, Figure 1). For the 23-year period (1990–2012), 131,096 strikes were reported to the FAA. Birds were involved in 97.0 percent of the reported strikes, terrestrial mammals in 2.2 percent, bats in 0.6 percent and reptiles in 0.1 percent (Table 1).

Although the number of reported strikes has steadily increased, it is important to note that the overall number of reported damaging strikes has actually declined since 2000 (Figure 2). This decline in damaging strikes has occurred in the commercial aviation sector. The number and rate (number per 100,000 movements) of damaging strikes with commercial aircraft has declined 25 percent and 12 percent, respectively, from 2000 to 2012 (Table 2, Figure 3). Most of this decline has occurred in the airport environment (strikes occurring on departure or arrival at ≤500 feet above ground level [AGL]). The number of damaging strikes with commercial aircraft at ≤500 feet AGL has declined 35 percent from 353 in 2000 to 228 in 2012 (Figure 4). In contrast, the number of damaging strikes with commercial aircraft at >500 feet AGL has increased slightly from 142 in 2000

One of the activities of Bird Strike Committee–USA, an organization of government and aviation industry members, is to promote reporting of wildlife strikes. In 2012, 86 percent of the 10,726 strike reports were filed electronically (Table 4). Photo, R. Young, Florida Aviation Network.

to 151 in 2012. These declines in damaging strikes for commercial aviation in the airport environment have occurred in spite of an increase in populations of hazardous wildlife species (Dolbeer 2000, Dolbeer and Eschenfelder 2003) and demonstrate progress in wildlife hazard management programs at airports certificated for passenger traffic under 14 CFR Part 139 regulations (Dolbeer 2011).

The rate of damaging strikes with General Aviation (GA) aircraft has gradually risen from 0.17 in 1990 to 0.32 in 2012 (Table 3, Figure 3). There has not been a decline in damaging strikes in the airport environment (at <500 feet AGL) for General Aviation aircraft (Figure 4). Between 2011 and 2012, GA aircraft strike reports increased at almost twice the rate (11 percent) than the remainder of civil aircraft strike reporting.

METHODS OF REPORTING STRIKES

In 2012, 86 percent and 4 percent of the 10,726 strike reports were filed using the electronic and paper versions, respectively, of FAA Form 5200-7, *Bird/Other Wildlife Strike Report*. Since the online version of this form became available in April 2001, use of the electronic reporting system has climbed dramatically. The remaining 10 percent of strike reports filed in 2012 were obtained from various sources (Table 4).

SOURCE OF REPORTS

In 2012, airport operations personnel filed 60 percent of the strike reports (including "Carcass Found" reports), followed by pilots (23 percent), airlines operations personnel (11 percent), Air Traffic Control personnel (4 percent), and other (1 percent, Table 5). In 2012, about 86 percent of the reported strikes involved commercial aircraft; the remainder involved business, private, and government aircraft (Table 6).

The number of USA airports with strikes reported has increased steadily from 332 in 1990 to a record 643 in 2012 (Table 7, Figure 5). The 643 airports with strikes reported in 2012 were comprised of 387 airports certificated for passenger service under 14 CFR Part 139 and 256 General Aviation airports. From 1990–2012, strikes have been reported from 1,771 USA airports. In addition, strikes involving USA-registered aircraft were reported from 273 foreign airports in 1990–2012.

A Eurocopter EC 130, en route at dusk to pick up a medical patient in Tennessee, hit a mallard at 2,000 feet AGL, shattering the right windshield, Feb 2012. The pilot made an emergency landing in a field. Of the 1,395 strikes involving helicopters from 1990–2012, 390 (28%) were on medical transport missions; 72% of the medical transport strikes occurred at dusk or night. Photo, Paris (TN) Post-Intelligencer.

TIMING OF OCCURRENCE AND PHASE OF FLIGHT OF STRIKES

From 1990–2012, most bird strikes (52 percent) occurred between July and October (Figure 6) which is when birds are migrating and populations are at their annual peak following the nesting season. Sixty-two percent of bird strikes occurred during the day and 29 percent at night (Table 8). Almost twice as many strikes (60 percent of total) occurred during the landing (descent, approach, or landing roll) phase of flight compared to 37 percent during takeoff run and climb (Table 9).

Similar to the pattern shown with birds, most terrestrial mammal strikes occurred during between July and November; with 30 percent of deer strikes concentrated in October-November (Figure 6). Most terrestrial mammal strikes (63 percent) occurred at night (Table 8). As with birds, almost twice as many strikes (64 percent of total) occurred during the landing (final approach or landing roll) phase of flight compared to 34 percent during takeoff run and climb (Table 9).

HEIGHT ABOVE GROUND LEVEL (AGL) OF STRIKES

Bird strikes with commercial aircraft. From 1990–2012, about 41 percent of bird strikes with commercial aircraft occurred when the aircraft was at 0 feet AGL, 72 percent occurred at 500 feet or less AGL, and 92 percent occurred at or below 3,500 feet AGL (Table 10). Less than 1 percent of bird strikes occurred above 9,500 feet AGL. Above 500 feet AGL, the number of reported strikes declined consistently by 34 percent for each 1,000-foot gain in height (Figure 7). The record height for a reported bird strike involving a commercial aircraft in USA was 31,300 feet AGL.

Strikes occurring above 500 feet AGL had a greater probability of causing damage to the aircraft compared to strikes at 500 feet or less. Although only 28 percent of the reported strikes were above 500 feet AGL, these strikes represented 43 percent of the damaging strikes (Table 10, Figure 8).

Bird strikes with general aviation (GA) aircraft. From 1990–2012, about 37 percent of the bird strikes with GA aircraft occurred when the aircraft was at 0 feet AGL, 74 percent occurred at 500 feet or less AGL, and 97 percent occurred at or below 3,500 feet AGL (Table 11). Less than 1 percent of bird strikes occurred above 7,500 feet AGL. Above 500 feet AGL, the number of reported strikes

A Canada goose penetrated the radome of a CLRJ-200 at 1,700 feet AGL during initial climb out of an eastern U.S. airport, Dec 2012. The nose/radome is the aircraft component most frequently struck by birds. Photo courtesy of airport.

declined consistently by 42 percent for each 1,000-foot gain in height (Figure 7). The record height for a reported bird strike involving a GA aircraft in USA was 24,000 feet AGL.

Strikes occurring above 500 feet AGL had an even greater probability of causing damage to GA aircraft compared to strikes at 500 feet or less than was shown for commercial aircraft above. Although only 26 percent of the reported strikes were above 500 feet AGL, these strikes represented 48 percent of the damaging strikes (Table 11, Figure 8).

Terrestrial mammal strikes. As expected, terrestrial mammal strikes predominately occurred at 0 feet AGL; however, 9 percent of the reported strikes occurred when the aircraft was in the air immediately after lift-off or before touch down (e.g., when an aircraft struck a deer with the landing gear, Table 9).

AIRCRAFT COMPONENTS DAMAGED

The aircraft components most commonly reported as struck by birds from 1990–2012 were the nose/radome, windshield, engine, wing/rotor, and fuselage (Table 12). Aircraft engines were the component most frequently reported as being damaged by bird strikes (30 percent of all damaged components). There were 14,322 strike events in which a total of 15,013 engines were reported as struck (13,656 events with one engine struck, 647 with two engines struck, 13 with three engines struck, and 6 with four engines struck). In 4,069 damaging bird-strike events involving engines, a total of 4,206 engines was damaged (3,935 events with one engine damaged, 132 with two engines damaged, 1 with three engines damaged, and 1 with four engines damaged).

A CLRJ 200 struck a flock of snow geese at 7,000 feet AGL during descent about 30 miles from an east coast airport, Dec 2012. The radome, fuselage and a wing sustained damage, and flight crew visibility was impaired. An emergency was declared and the aircraft landed safely. The aircraft was out of service 38 days for repairs. Photo courtesy of airport.

Aircraft components most commonly reported as struck by terrestrial mammals were the landing gear, propeller, "other", and wing/rotor. These same components ranked highest for the parts most often reported as damaged by mammals (Table 12).

REPORTED DAMAGE

For the 127,212 strike reports involving birds from 1990–2012, 11,881 (9 percent) indicated damage to the aircraft (Table 13). When classified by level of damage, 6,403 (5 percent) indicated the aircraft suffered minor damage; 3,003 (2 percent) indicated the aircraft suffered substantial damage; 2,443 (2 percent) reported an uncertain level of damage; and 32 reports (less than 1 percent) indicated the aircraft was destroyed as a result of the strike (Table 13).

For the 2,946 terrestrial mammal strikes reported, 997 (34 percent) indicated damage to the aircraft. When classified by level of damage, 516 (18 percent) indicated the aircraft suffered minor damage; 386 (13 percent) indicated the aircraft suffered substantial damage; 67 (2 percent) reported an uncertain level of damage; and 28 (1 percent) indicated the aircraft was destroyed as a result of the strike (Table 13). Not surprisingly, a much higher percentage of terrestrial mammal strikes (34 percent) resulted in aircraft damage than did bird strikes (9 percent). Deer (1,037 strikes, of which 877 caused damage; Table 17) were involved in 35 percent of the strikes and 88 percent of the damaging strikes involving terrestrial mammals.

Although the percentage of bird strikes with reported damage has averaged 9 percent for the 23-year period, this number has declined from 20 percent in 1990 to 5 to 6 percent in 2009–2012 (Figure 9). For terrestrial mammals (23-year average of 34 percent), the decline has been from 83 percent in 1990 to 16 percent in 2012.

Falconers successfully use Harris's hawks at Dallas-Ft. Worth International Airport (DFW) in winter to disperse flocks of great-tailed grackles attempting to roost at night in live oak trees in the terminal area. Photo, R. Dolbeer, June 2012.

REPORTED NEGATIVE EFFECT-ON-FLIGHT

A negative effect-on-flight was reported in 7 percent and 23 percent of the bird and terrestrial mammal strike reports, respectively (Table 14). Precautionary/emergency landing after striking wildlife was the most commonly reported negative effect (4,538 incidents, 4 percent of strike reports). These precautionary landings included 171 incidents in which the pilot jettisoned fuel (45), burned fuel in a circling pattern (46) to lighten aircraft weight, or made an overweight landing (80, Table 15, Figure 10). In the 45 reported incidents in which fuel was jettisoned, an average of 90,306 pounds (13,280 gallons) of fuel was dumped per incident (range 515–39,706 gallons).

Aborted takeoff after striking wildlife was the second most commonly reported negative effect (1,990 incidents, 2 percent of strike reports, Table 14). These negative incidents included 836 aborted takeoffs in which the pilot initiated the abort at an aircraft speed of 80 knots (92 miles per hour) or greater (Table 16, Figure 11). In 141 incidents, the aircraft speed at the time of abort was 120 knots (138 miles per hour) or greater.

WILDLIFE SPECIES INVOLVED IN STRIKES

Table 17 shows the number of reported strikes, strikes causing damage, strikes having an negative effect-on-flight, strikes involving >1 animal, the reported aircraft down time, and the reported costs by identified wildlife species, 1990–2012. This information can be useful in comparing the relative hazard level of bird and other wildlife species encountered during Wildlife Hazard Assessments at airports and in the development of priorities for Wildlife Hazard Management Plans (see also Table 19).

An Embraer 190 struck two Canada geese at 100 feet AGL on departure from an eastern airport in April 2012. The pilot declared an emergency and returned safely to the airport. The seal of the windshield was damaged. This was 1 of 50 Canada goose strikes reported for civil aircraft in 2012. Photo courtesy of airline.

Of the 127,212 reported bird strikes, 45,295 (36 percent) identified the bird to exact species and an additional 17,126 strikes (13 percent) identified the bird at least to species group (e.g., gull, hawk, duck). Species identification has improved from less than 20 percent in the early 1990s to 56 percent in 2012 (Figure 12). In all, 482 species of birds have been identified as struck by aircraft, and 222 of these species were reported as causing damage, 1990–2012.

Gulls (15 percent), doves/pigeons (15 percent), raptors (13 percent), and waterfowl (7 percent) were the most frequently struck bird groups (Table 18). Gulls were involved in 2.2 times more strikes than waterfowl (9,252 and 4,137, respectively). Waterfowl, however, were involved in 1.3 times more damaging strikes (1,767 or 30 percent of all damaging strikes in which the bird type was identified) than were gulls (1,321 or 22 percent of all damaging strikes in which the bird type was identified). Gulls and pigeons/doves were responsible for the greatest number of bird strikes (2,021 and 1,990, respectively) that involved multiple birds.

The most frequently struck terrestrial mammals were Artiodactyls— primarily deer (37 percent)— and Carnivores— primarily coyotes (35 percent) (Tables 17, 18). Artiodactyls were responsible for 92 percent of the mammal strikes that resulted in damage and 77 percent of the mammal strikes that involved multiple animals. In all, 42,

15 and 11 identified species of terrestrial mammals, bats, and reptiles, respectively, were reported struck; 22, 2, and 2 identified species of these respective wildlife taxa caused damage to aircraft (Table 17).

HAZARD LEVEL OF WILDLIFE SPECIES

Table 19 ranks the hazard level of 86 species of birds and 10 species of terrestrial mammals with 50 or more reported strikes (from Table 17). The ranking is based on a composite of the percent of strikes causing damage, major damage, and a negative effect-on-flight. For birds, the hazard rating ranged from 53 percent for snow geese to ≤1 percent for 30 species. For terrestrial mammals, the hazard rating ranged from 58 percent for mule deer to ≤1 percent for black-tailed jackrabbits, Virginia opossums, and striped skunks. This ranking provides a means to objectively estimate the relative hazard level of species to aircraft operations and can be useful in prioritizing management actions at airports to mitigate risk from wildlife (Dolbeer and Wright 2009, DeVault et al. 2011).

Portland International Airport (PDX) is using landscape plantings to create visual barriers to discourage Canada geese from grazing in open areas on street-side airport property. This is an example of the creative approaches being implemented nationwide to mitigate the risk of strikes with Canada geese, one of the most hazardous bird species. Photo, Port of Portland, 2012.

Table 20 lists the mean hazard level and hazard level ranking (1 to 86 from Table 19) for the 25 bird species most frequently struck by civil aircraft, 1990–2012. Mourning doves were by far the most frequently struck species (5,362 strikes) followed by American kestrels, European starlings, killdeer, rock pigeons, and barn swallows with 2,303 to 3,236 strikes each. Fortunately, only two of the 25 most frequently struck species (Canada geese and turkey vultures) ranked in the top 10 (out of 86) most hazardous bird species (Table 19).

HUMAN FATALITIES AND INJURIES DUE TO WILDLIFE STRIKES

For the 23-year period, reports were received of 10 wildlife strikes that resulted in 24 human fatalities (Table 21). Five of these strikes resulting in 7 fatalities involved unidentified species of birds. Red-tailed hawks (8 fatalities), American white pelicans (5), Canada geese (2), white-tailed deer (1), and brown-pelicans (1) were responsible for the other 17 fatalities. Reports were received of 211 strikes that resulted in 276 human injuries (Table 21). Waterfowl (ducks and geese; 51 strikes, 58 humans injured), vultures (31 strikes, 38 injuries), and deer (20 strikes, 29 injuries) caused 102

(59 percent) of the 172 strikes resulting in injuries in which the species or species group was identified.

AIRCRAFT DESTROYED DUE TO WILDLIFE STRIKES

For the 23-year period, reports were received of 60 aircraft destroyed or damaged beyond repair due to wildlife strikes (Tables 13, 22). The majority (38; 63 percent) were small (≤2,250 kg maximum takeoff mass) general aviation (GA) aircraft. Terrestrial mammals (primarily white-tailed deer) were responsible for 27 (45 percent) of the incidents. Canada geese (5 incidents) and vultures (3 incidents) were responsible for 40 percent of the 20 incidents involving birds in which the species or species group was identified.

Forty (67 percent) of the 60 wildlife strikes resulting in a destroyed aircraft occurred at general aviation (GA) airports, 12 occurred "en-route", 6 occurred at USA airports certificated for passenger service under 14 CFR Part 139, and 2 occurred at a foreign airport certificated for passenger service (Table 22). GA airports, often located in rural areas with inadequate fencing to exclude large mammals, face unique challenges in mitigating wildlife risks to aviation (DeVault et al. 2008; Dolbeer et al. 2008).

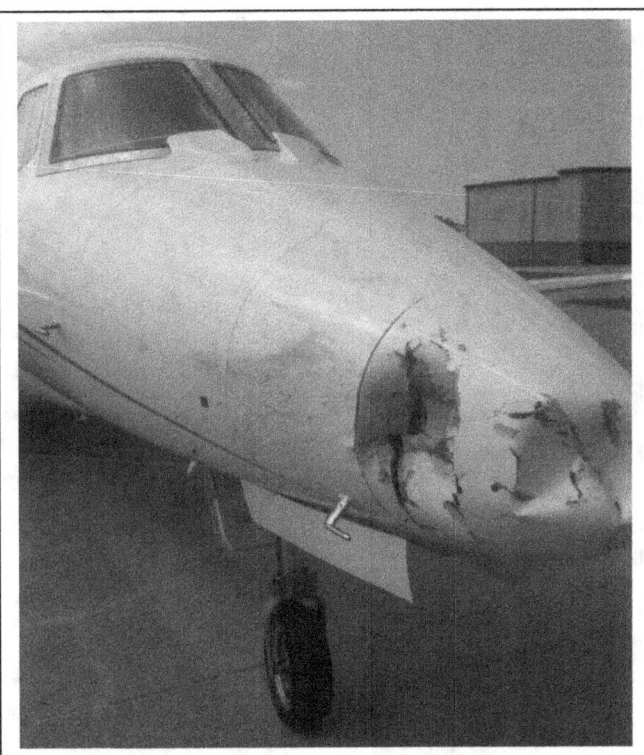

A C560 on approach to a Midwestern airport struck a soaring turkey vulture at 1,500 feet AGL in May 2012. The radome was damaged and parts of the bird were ingested into the #2 engine. The aircraft landed safely. Costs of repairs exceeded $200,000; the aircraft was out of service for 2 months. Photo courtesy of operator.

ECONOMIC LOSSES DUE TO WILDLIFE STRIKES

Of the 20,216 reports from 1990–2012 that indicated the strike had an adverse effect on the aircraft and/or flight, 6,703 provided an estimate of the aircraft downtime (815,997 hours, mean = 121.7 hours/incident, Tables 17, 23). Regarding monetary losses, 3,262 reports provided an estimate of direct aircraft repair costs ($571.4 million, mean = $175,177/incident), and 2,092 reports gave an estimate of other monetary losses ($68.0 million, mean = $32,495/incident)[1]. Other monetary losses include such expenses as lost revenue, the cost of putting passengers in hotels, re-scheduling aircraft, and flight cancellations.

[1] Costs from years prior to 2012 are inflation-adjusted to 2012 U.S. dollars.

Analysis of 14 groups of strike reports from 3 Part 139 airports certificated for passenger service and 3 airlines for the years 1991-2004 indicated that 11 to 21 percent of all strikes were reported to the FAA (Cleary et al. 2005, Wright and Dolbeer 2005). An independent analysis of strike data for a certificated airport in Hawaii in the 1990s indicated a similar reporting rate (Linnell et al. 1999). Analyses of strike data from 2004–2008 indicated strike reporting at Part 139 airports had improved to 39 percent (Dolbeer 2009). Strike reporting for general aviation (GA) aircraft is estimated at less than 5 percent (Dolbeer et al. 2008, Dolbeer 2009). In addition to the underreporting of strikes, only 33 percent of the 20,216 reports from 1990–2012 indicating an adverse effect provided estimates of aircraft downtime, 16 percent provided estimates of direct costs, and 10 percent provided estimates of other (indirect) costs (Tables 23, 24).

The pilot of a Pilatus PC-12/45 saw a large bird flying toward the aircraft at 6,000 feet on departure from a Florida airport in Sep 2012. The bird penetrated the fuselage. Remains were identified as an anhinga by the Smithsonian Feather Lab. From 1990-2012, 25 strikes involving anhinga, 12 of which caused damage, were reported for civil aircraft (Table 17). Photo by L. Hernandez.

Furthermore, many reports providing cost estimates were filed before aircraft damage and downtime had been fully assessed. As a result, the information on the number of strikes and associated costs compiled (summarized by species of wildlife struck in Table 17) is believed to underestimate the magnitude of the problem.

Assuming (1) all 20,216 reported wildlife strikes that had an adverse effect on the aircraft and/or flight engendered similar amounts of downtime and/or monetary losses and (2) that these reports are all of the damaging strikes that occurred, then at a minimum, wildlife strikes annually cost the USA civil aviation industry, on average, 116,635 hours of aircraft downtime and $191 million in monetary losses ($155 million in direct costs and $36 million in other costs), 1990–2012, (Table 24).

Further, if we assume that the 20,216 reported strikes indicating an adverse effect represent, on average, 20 percent of the total strikes that occurred with commercial and GA aircraft from 1990–2012, the annual cost of wildlife strikes to the USA civil aviation industry is estimated to be 583,175 hours of aircraft downtime and $957 million in direct and other monetary losses (Table 23).

CONCLUSIONS

This analysis of 23 years of strike data reveals the magnitude and nature of wildlife strikes with civil aircraft in the USA, and documents that progress is being made in reducing damaging strikes. Although wildlife strikes continue to pose a significant economic and safety risk for civil aviation in the USA, management actions to mitigate the risk have been implemented at many airports in the past decade (e.g., Wenning et al. 2004, DeFusco et al. 2005, Dolbeer 2006a, Human Wildlife Conflicts Journal 2009, Human-Wildlife Interactions Journal 2011, Dolbeer 2011). These efforts are likely responsible for the general decline in reported strikes with damage from 2000–2012 (Table 1, Figures 2, 3, 4, 9 and Dolbeer 2011) in spite of continued increases in populations of many large bird species. For example, USDA Wildlife Services biologists provided assistance at 772 airports nationwide in 2012 to mitigate wildlife risks to aviation compared to only 42 airports in 1991 and 193 in 1998 (Begier and Dolbeer 2013). However, much work remains to be done to reduce wildlife strikes.

To address the problem, airport managers first need to assess the wildlife hazards on their airports with the help of qualified airport biologists (FAA Advisory Circular 150/5200-36A). They then must take appropriate actions, under the guidance of professional biologists trained in wildlife damage management at airports, to minimize the risks posed by wildlife. Management actions should be prioritized based on the hazard level of species (Table 19) observed in the aircraft operating area. The manual *Wildlife Hazard Management at Airports* (Cleary and Dolbeer 2005) provides guidance to airport personnel and biologists for conducting wildlife hazard assessments and in developing and implementing wildlife hazard management plans. PDF versions of the manual are available online in English, Spanish, and French at http://wildlife.faa.gov.

Management efforts to reduce the risks of bird strikes have primarily focused on airports since various historical analyses of bird strike data for civil aviation have indicated the majority of strikes occur in this environment (during take-off and landing at ≤500 feet above ground level). Dolbeer (2011) conducted a trend analysis of bird strike data involving commercial air carriers that indicated the percentage of all strikes that occurred at more than 500 feet increased significantly from about 25 percent in 1990 to 30 percent in 2009. The percentage of all damaging strikes that occurred at more than 500 feet increased at a greater rate, from about 37 percent in the early 1990s to 45 percent in 2005 to 2009. Dolbeer (2011) also examined trends in strike rates (strikes/1

As part of integrated programs to mitigate the risk of bird strikes, various airports in the USA are planting open areas with grasses, such as endophytic fescues, that are less palatable to geese, rodents and insects than traditionally planted grass varieties. Researchers at USDA are evaluating these plantings. Photo, USDA.

million commercial aircraft movements) for strikes occurring at less than or equal to and more than 500 feet. From 1990 to 2009, the damaging strike rate at more than 500 feet increased from about 2.5 to 4.0, whereas the damaging strike rate for strikes at 500 or less feet has remained stable since 2000. The successful mitigation efforts at airports that have reduced damaging strikes in recent years, which must be sustained, have done little to reduce strikes outside the airport such as occurred with US Airways Flight 1549 in 2009 (Dolbeer 2011).

Bird-detecting radar is being evaluated at Dallas–Ft. Worth and other airports in the USA as part of research and development efforts to further mitigate the risk of bird strikes. Photo, R. Dolbeer, June 2012.

To address this trend in strikes above 500 feet, the general public and aviation community must first widen its view of wildlife management to consider habitats and land uses within 5 miles of airports. Wetlands, dredge-spoil containment areas, municipal solid waste landfills, and wildlife refuges can attract hazardous wildlife. Such land uses, as discussed in FAA Advisory Circular 150/5200-33B, *Hazardous Wildlife Attractants on or Near Airports,* are often incompatible with aviation safety and should either be prohibited near airports or designed and operated in a manner that minimizes the attraction of hazardous wildlife. Second, on-going research and mitigation efforts to further develop and incorporate avian radar and bird migration forecasting and to study avian sensory perception to enhance aircraft detection and avoidance by birds should be maintained (e.g., Blackwell et al. 2012). Third, Federal guidance on wildlife hazards at airports should continue to be reviewed, and where necessary revised, to incorporate new information about wildlife hazards and wildlife strike reporting trends. Finally, there continues to be a need for increased and more detailed reporting of information about wildlife strikes, such as species identification and number of wildlife struck, time and altitude of strike, and damage costs.

Dolbeer (2009) concluded that strike reporting at Part 139 airports has increased from about 20 percent in the 1990s to 39 percent in 2004 to 2008. The percentage of bird strikes in which the bird was identified to species has improved from less than 20 percent in the early 1990s to 56 percent in 2012. Overall, only 17 percent of strike reports indicating an adverse effect on the aircraft or flight provided at least a partial estimate of economic losses resulting from the strike, 1990–2012.

REPORTING A STRIKE AND IDENTIFYING SPECIES OF WILDLIFE STRUCK

Pilots, airport operations, aircraft maintenance personnel, and anyone else having knowledge of a strike should report the incident to the FAA using FAA Form 5200-7. Strikes can be reported electronically via the internet (http://wildlife.faa.gov) or Form 5200-7 can be accessed and printed for mailing in reports.

It is important to include as much information as possible on FAA Form 5200-7. All reports are carefully screened to identify duplicate reports prior to entry in the database. Multiple reports of the same incident are combined and often provide a more complete record of the strike event than would be possible if just one report were filed.

The identification of the exact species struck (e.g., ring-billed gull, Canada goose, mallard, mourning dove, or red-tailed hawk as opposed to gull, goose, duck, dove, or hawk) is particularly important. This species information is critical for biologists developing wildlife risk management programs at airports and for engineers working on airworthiness standards because a problem that cannot be measured or defined cannot be solved. Bird strike remains that cannot be identified by airport personnel can often be identified by a local biologist trained in ornithology or by sending feather and other remains in a sealed plastic bag (with FAA Form 5200-7) to:

Material sent via Express Mail Service:	Material sent via U.S. Postal Service:
Feather Identification Lab	Feather Identification Lab
Smithsonian Institution NMNH	Smithsonian Institution NMNH
E600 MRC 116	E600 MRC 116
10th & Constitution Ave. NW	PO Box 37012
Washington DC 20560-0116	Washington DC 20013-7012
(label package "safety investigation material")	(not recommended for priority cases)
Phone:202-633-0787 or 202-633-0791	

The number of bird strike cases processed by the Smithsonian Feather Identification Lab for the FAA (civil aviation) in 2012 was 2,072 with 2,190 separate identifications of species (some cases involved remains from multiple impact points). This compares to 1,580 cases in 2011 and 1,268 cases in 2010 (Dove et al. 2013). In addition, the Lab processed 4,058 identifications for the U.S. Air Force and 671 identifications for the Navy (not discussed in this report). DNA analysis was used in 1,237 (56 percent) of all identifications for civil aviation to identify, supplement, or verify traditional identification methods.

Whenever possible, reporters should send whole feathers as diagnostic characteristics are often found in the downy barbules at the feather base. Wings, as well as breast and tail feathers, should be sent whenever possible. Beaks, feet, bones, and talons are also useful diagnostic materials. Even blood smears can provide material for DNA analysis

(Dove et al. 2008). Do not send entire bird carcasses through the mail. However, photographs of the carcasses can be very useful supplemental documentation.

Guidelines for Collecting Bird Strike Material

- Always include any feather material available.
- Include copy of report (FAA 5200-7).
- Always secure all remains in re-sealable plastic bag.

Feathers:
- <u>Whole Bird</u> – Pluck a variety of feathers (breast, back, wing, tail)

- <u>Partial Bird</u> – Collect a variety of feathers with color or pattern

- <u>Feathers only</u> – Send all material available. Do not cut feathers from the bird (downy part at the base of the feathers is needed). Do not use any sticky substance (no tape or glue).

Tissue/blood ("Snarge"):
- <u>Dry material</u> – Scrape or wipe off into a clean re-closeable bag **or** wipe area with pre-packaged alcohol wipe **or** spray with alcohol to loosen material then wipe with clean cloth/gauze. (Do not use water, bleach, or other cleansers; they destroy DNA.)

- <u>Fresh material</u> – Wipe area with alcohol wipe and/or clean cloth/gauze **or** apply fresh tissue/blood to an FTA® DNA collecting card.

FTA® Micro Card and Sterile Applicators

If you send a lot of fresh blood/ tissue samples for DNA identification, you may want to consider getting Whatman FTA® DNA cards. The material is sampled with a sterile applicator and placed onto the surface of the card that "fixes" the DNA in the sample. For more information on ordering these items contact the Feather Lab.

Note: If you only occasionally send blood/ tissue samples, a paper towel with alcohol or alcohol wipe is still a good option for this type of material.

Additional information on sending bird remains to the Smithsonian is available at http://wildlife.faa.gov.

FAA ACTIVITIES FOR MITIGATING WILDLIFE STRIKES

In 2012, the FAA continued a multifaceted approach for mitigating wildlife strikes. This included continuing a robust research program, making improvements to the NWSD and outreach, incorporating new technology to increase and simplify strike reporting, and providing Airport Improvement Program (AIP) funding to airports to conduct Wildlife Hazard Assessments (WHAs) and develop Wildlife Hazard Management Plans (WHMPs).

STRIKE REPORTING

As there is still room for improvement, the FAA retooled the existing wildlife strike database website (http://wildlife.faa.gov) to make it more user-friendly and to allow more advanced data mining. Search fields enable users to find data on specific airports, airlines, aircraft and engine types, as well as damage incurred, date of strike, species struck, and state without having to download the entire database. Separately, the FAA provides in-depth wildlife guidance at http://www.faa.gov/airports/airport_safety/wildlife.

This guidance includes Advisory Circulars and Certalerts, FAA National Wildlife Strike Database analysis reports, the manual *Wildlife Hazard Management at Airports,* Airport Cooperative Research Program (ACRP) wildlife reports, hazardous wildlife mitigation and habitat attractants, Bird Hazard Mitigation Systems (e.g., AHAS and BAM), Frequently Asked Questions and Answers on Wildlife Strikes, and more.

The FAA also developed software to make strike reporting easier. Now, anyone who needs to report a wildlife strike can do so via the new web site or their mobile devices at http://www.faa.gov/mobile. When airline and airport employees report a wildlife strike, the information is automatically sent to the FAA's wildlife strike database.

The FAA continued to distribute the latest *Report Wildlife Strikes* awareness poster throughout 2012. Overall, 24,000 posters have been distributed to more than 4,000 Part 139 airports, General Aviation airports, aviation flight schools and the aviation

The FAA distributed 12,000 new Report Wildlife Strike posters to more than 4,000 Part 139 and General Aviation airports and the aviation industry.

industry in the last two years. The renewal of strike awareness posters is one of several outreach efforts to improve strike reporting and safety at certificated and General Aviation airports. As an extension to the mobile application software developed by the FAA to make strike reporting easier, the FAA also placed a QR code on the bottom of the 2011–2012 "Report Wildlife Strikes" poster, which allows anyone to report a wildlife strike via the web or their personal data devices. Outreach materials such as informational placards and quick-reference thumb guides are also being developed for distribution.

In August 2011, Embry Riddle Aeronautical University (ERAU) conducted a survey to collect information from wildlife strike reporters. The study was initiated through the interagency agreement between the FAA and USDA and collaborative efforts with ERAU. The goals of the survey were to learn more about the demographics of strike submitters, determine how people learned about strike reporting, and collect feedback on the strike submission form and on ways to enhance the system. Subsequent recommendations to improve outreach and the ease and accessibility of strike reporting have been implemented while methods to improve communication, feedback, cooperative efforts between agencies and reporting parties and training are being investigated. Specific recommendations addressed or initiated in 2012 included:

1. Cooperation with Other Organizations – Avoid duplication of reporting.
2. Communication and Feedback – Improve communication throughout aviation industry and provide regular feedback to strike reporters.
3. Wildlife Strike Reporting Form Changes
4. Multiple Versions of Strike Forms – Provide specific strike form relevant to individual reporting strike.
5. Website Changes – Dynamic online form, prepopulated fields and increased availability of website linked to aviation industry websites.
6. Training and Education – More information regarding what and how to collect strike remains and report the strike.
7. Funding – Prepaid kits addressed to the Smithsonian.
8. Miscellaneous – Add iPhone / iPad application and / or toll free number to report strikes.

Airports must often integrate diverse management procedures that require special permits to mitigate a wide range of wildlife hazards. The presence of Federal and State threatened and endangered species may require a coexistence mandate incompatible with the airport's primary function of a safe environment for aviation. Examples of protected species documented on airports include Sage Grouse, Streaked Horned Lark, Bald Eagles, Gopher Tortoises and the Burrowing Owls depicted above from two different airports. Photos courtesy of Jim Price.

WILDLIFE HAZARD MITIGATION RESEARCH

For the last 17 years, the FAA and the USDA have conducted a research program to make airports safer by reducing the risks of aircraft-wildlife collisions. The research efforts designed to improve wildlife management techniques and practices on and near airports include:

- Alternatives to habitat management to reduce attraction to hazardous species
- Techniques for controlling species by restricting access to attractive features like storm water ponds
- Technologies for harassing and deterring hazardous species
- Evaluation of avian radar systems for detecting and tracking birds on or near airports
- Aircraft-mounted alternating, pulse lights to enhance aircraft detection and deter wildlife strikes

Avian or Bird Radar Technology

In 2001, the FAA began working with the U.S. Air Force to develop a radar system for detecting and tracking birds on or near airports. In 2006, the FAA refocused the radar research to evaluate the capability of commercially available, low-cost, portable radars to reliably detect and track birds on or near airports.

The Center of Excellence for Airport Technology (CEAT) at the University of Illinois has served as the FAA's research partner for the performance assessments of bird radar. The initial avian radar systems have involved Accipiter Radar Technologies Inc. and were deployed at Seattle-Tacoma and Whidbey Island Naval Station in 2007, Chicago O'Hare in 2009, and John F. Kennedy and Dallas–Fort Worth in 2010.

Additional evaluations have continued through FAA's multi-year agreement with USDA who teamed up with the National Center of Atmospheric Research (NCAR) and Indiana State University to further evaluate the performance of bird radar systems. The effort brings together experts in wildlife biology, ornithology, radar engineering, and system integration from government, industry, and academia to evaluate the MERLIN Avian Radar System by DeTect, Inc., one of several radar systems used to detect birds at and near airports. The assessment effort is part of the FAA's overall investigation into the effectiveness of commercially available avian radar detection systems at U.S. civil airports when used in conjunction with other known wildlife management and control techniques. Though it is well established that radar can detect wild birds, there is little published information concerning the accuracy and detection capabilities related to range, altitude, target size, and effects of weather for avian radar systems. NWRC researchers are leading the effort involving experts from the National Center for Atmospheric Research and several universities. Efforts involve (1) a technical evaluation of the candidate radar system, including sensor components and associated data delivery systems, (2) field evaluations of system accuracy using remote controlled aircraft and wild birds, (3) an assessment of the integration of radar technology with other, more traditional aspects of wildlife hazard management at airports, and (4) a behavioral study on the potential effects of radar energy on bird behavior.

In November, 2010, the FAA published a performance specification in the form of an Advisory Circular 150/5220-25, *Airport Avian Radar Systems*, which airports can use to competitively purchase bird radar systems. The guidelines provide the operational considerations of acquiring and using the technology to enhance wildlife hazard mitigation practices on civil airports. Under some circumstances, procurement of bird radar systems may be eligible for funding under the FAA's Airport Improvement Program (AIP). The FAA will continue to evaluate commercially available avian radars and emerging sensor technologies. A new research effort began at the end of 2011 and continued through 2012 that will examine the feasibility and practicality of pilots and air traffic controllers using bird radar data.

WILDLIFE HAZARD ASSESSMENTS AND WILDLIFE HAZARD MANAGEMENT PLANS

The FAA has encouraged all certificated airports to conduct WHAs and develop WHMPs regardless if they have experienced a triggering event under Part 139 To date, 100 percent of Part 139 airports have completed a WHA, are in the process of conducting a WHA, or have taken a Federal grant to conduct a WHA. Wildlife hazard assessments will allow an airport to:

The FAA has developed specific guidance and outreach efforts targeting General Aviation airports to increase strike reporting.   Efforts are underway to have Site Visits or Wildlife Hazard Assessments conducted at each NPIAS GA airport. Photo courtesy of John Weller.

- Identify trends in wildlife use of the airport (habitat preferences, seasonal composition and abundance of wildlife species, geography of strikes, seasonality of strikes, time and phase of flight of strikes, etc.)
- Prevent future strikes through operational changes, habitat (attractant) modifications, customized harassment, and/ or species removal
- Evaluate the overall risk level of wildlife strikes and the efficacy of the airport's wildlife hazard mitigation program (e.g., determine redundancy of species specific hazards, monitor reduction of onsite damaging strikes, monitor wildlife program communication and response efficiency, and improve overall program through annual review)

A WHA provides fundamental wildlife and habitat information for an effective, airport-specific WHMP. The WHMP outlines a plan of action to minimize the risk to aviation safety, airport structures or equipment, or human health posed by populations of hazardous wildlife on and around an airport. To be effective, WHMPs must not only be fully implemented but routinely evaluated and modified to address an airport's changing environment, hazards and capabilities. The FAA supports completion of wildlife hazard assessments and wildlife hazard management plans by providing financial assistance from the AIP.

New guidance providing minimum acceptable standards for the conduct and development of WHAs and WHMPs was submitted for public comments in November 2012. Advisory Circular 150/5200-38, *Protocol for the Conduct and Review of Wildlife Hazard Site Visits, Wildlife Hazard Assessments, and Wildlife Hazard Management Plans,* details survey methodologies and frequency to better evaluate risk and ultimately mitigate hazards effectively. It will be issued to the public in 2013.

Wildlife Hazard Assessments at GA Airports

On March 4, 2008, a catastrophic wildlife strike involving a Cessna 500 Citation and an unknown number of migratory white pelicans resulted in five fatalities approximately four miles from a GA airport. Following the investigation, the NTSB provided the FAA Recommendation A-09-73:

> "Verify that all federally obligated general aviation airports that are located near woodlands, water, wetlands, or other wildlife attractants are complying with the requirements to perform wildlife hazard assessments as specified in Federal Aviation Administration Advisory Circular 150/5200-33B, Hazardous Wildlife Attractants On or Near Airports"

In response to this recommendation, the FAA initiated the modification of AC 150/5200-33B and grant assurances to clarify the responsibility of federally obligated National Plan of Integrated Airport System/ General Aviation (NPIAS/GA) airports, to conduct WHAs. The FAA continues to encourage federally obligated GA airports to conduct WHAs and Wildlife Hazard Site Visits (WHSV) and has established a program and schedule that outlines the implementation of the new processes. It will take several years to complete WHAs and

A Western grebe shattered the windshield of an Ameriflight BE-99, injuring the pilot of Flight 2850. The strike occurred on November 4, 2010, at 4,200 feet AGL and approximately 20 miles from the airport.

WHSVs at the more than 2,700 GA airports. To assist the airports in conducting the WHAs, we will make AIP grant funds available to them.

OTHER ACTIVITIES

Mitigating Strikes at GA Airports

The FAA funded and assisted with the development of two new Airport Cooperative Research Program (ACRP) reports to aid General Aviation airports with the mitigation of wildlife hazards. Two-thousand seven hundred and seventy copies of ACRP Report 32, *Guidebook for Addressing Aircraft/ Wildlife Hazards at General Aviation Airports,* and ACRP Synthesis 23, *Bird Harassment, Repellent, and Deterrent Techniques for Use on and Near Airports,* were distributed in October 2011 and early 2012 to all federally obligated National Plan of Integrated Airport System (NPIAS) General Aviation airports. The reports, published in 2010 and 2011 respectively, provide practical guidance and specific techniques on how to address wildlife strikes at airports with a specific emphasis on the general aviation community.

Certalert No. 13-01, *Federal and State Depredation Permit Assistance,* issued in January 2013 provided assistance to airport operators with the acquisition of Federal or State depredation permits. The Certalert supplied users with state fish, wildlife and natural resource agency web sites, contact information for USDA and United States Fish And Wildlife Service (USFWS) regional and state offices, USFWS Migratory Bird Permits Regulation 50 CFR § 21.41 and a copy of USFWS Migratory Bird Depredation Permit application form (Form 3-200-13).

Bird Strike Committee USA

The FAA cosponsors the Bird Strike Committee-USA as part of its continued public outreach and education effort to increase awareness within the aviation community about wildlife hazards. A Memorandum of Understanding between the FAA and the BSC-USA was signed May 2012 to formalize this cooperative relationship.

Commercial Aviation Safety Team (CAST)

In 2010, the FAA Airports Safety and Standards (AAS), USDA and the Air Transport Association requested that the Commercial Aviation Safety Team (CAST) formally charter a Joint Safety Analysis Team or similar effort to review the wildlife strike/ aviation problem. CAST determined that the Joint Implementation Measurement and Data Analysis Team (JIMDAT) group would track wildlife strikes and provide periodic monitoring reports to CAST concerning wildlife strikes.

During a February 2013 CAST meeting, CAST fully approved JIMDAT "Option 2" Birdstrike monitoring proposal. This included reporting fatality risk values at appropriate intervals and trending egregious events to provide confidence. Egregious event categories to monitor are: A/C Controllability, Fire, Multiple Systems Damaged, High

Risk RTO, Loss of/Unreliable Cockpit Data, Cockpit Intrusion (Risk of Pilot Incapacitation), and Encountered Many Large Birds. Event categories were chosen by a SME panel as safety significant event precursors.

Performance Metrics

Starting in FY 2013, the FAA adopted the following performance metrics that will measure program efficacy under a voluntary strike reporting environment where the absolute number of bird strikes is not known. These three performance metrics allow the FAA to monitor multiple factors that affect strike reporting and overall strike reporting trends and the effectiveness of GA wildlife mitigation programs. To date, strike reporting trends continue to show an increase in overall reporting contrasted with an actual decline in damaging strikes within the airport environment (< 500 feet AGL) from 764 in 2000 to 606 in 2012. Further analysis of strike reporting trends will be completed in FY 2014 following completion of Metric 2.

- **Metric 1:** Monitor the ratio between the numbers of strikes with damage compared to total reported strikes. This ratio is independent of the total number of strikes reported and is a good measure of the effectiveness of overall mitigation procedures. We will use Fiscal Year (FY) 2010 as the baseline data and calculate the performance measure for FY 2011, FY 2012, and future years. The table below depicts the results of calculating the data for FYs 2010, 2011, and 2012.

	Total Strikes Reported	Damaging Strikes Reported	Percentage Damaging Strikes vs. Total Strikes
FY 10	9,920	598	6%
FY 11	10,123	541	5%
FY 12	10,726	606	5%

- **Metric 2:** Monitor estimated reporting rate of wildlife strikes. In FY 2014, we will update the Dolbeer study that estimated the 39 percent reporting rate to determine if our outreach efforts have increased the reporting rate. We will continue to update the study every 3 years thereafter.

- **Metric 3:** We will monitor the number of general aviation airport assessments or site visits initiated. This is an important metric as we are just starting an initiative to complete assessments or site visits at more than 2,700 general aviation airports. This initiative will run for more than 10 years, and it is important to track our progress. We are in the process of implementing procedures to collect data on GA airports conducting WHAs. The data will be included in the next report.

This page intentionally left blank

LITERATURE CITED

Begier, M. J., and R. A. Dolbeer. 2013. Protecting the flying public and minimizing economic losses within the aviation industry: technical, operational, and research assistance provided by USDA-APHIS-Wildlife Services to reduce wildlife hazards to aviation, Fiscal year 2012. Special report, U.S. Department of Agriculture, Animal and Plant Health Inspection Service, Wildlife Services. Washington, D.C., USA. 14 pages.

Biondi, K. M., J. L. Belant, J. A. Martin, T. L. DeVault, and G. Wang. 2011. White-tailed deer incidents with U.S. civil aircraft. Wildlife Society Bulletin 35(3):303–309.

Blackwell, B. F., T. L. DeVault ,T. W. Seamans, S. L. Lima, P. Baumhardt, and E. Fernández-Juricic. 2012. Exploiting avian vision with aircraft lighting to reduce bird strikes. Journal of Applied Ecology 49(4):758-766.

Burger, J. 1983. Jet aircraft noise and bird strikes: why more birds are being hit. Environmental Pollution (Series A) 30:143–152.

Cleary, E. C., and R. A. Dolbeer. 2005. Wildlife hazard management at airports, a manual for airport operators. Second edition. Federal Aviation Administration, Office of Airport Safety and Standards, Washington, D.C., USA. 348 pages. (http://wildlife.faa.gov).

Cleary, E. C., R. A. Dolbeer, and S. E. Wright. 2005. Wildlife strikes to civil aircraft in the United States, 1990-2004. U.S. Department of Transportation, Federal Aviation Administration, Office of Airport Safety and Standards, Serial Report No. 11. Washington, D.C., USA. 56 pages.

DeFusco, R. P., M. J. Hovan, J. T. Harper, and K. A. Heppard. 2005. North American Bird Strike Advisory System, Strategic Plan. Institute for Information Technology Applications, U.S. Air Force Academy, Colorado Springs, Colorado, USA. 31 pages.

DeVault, T.L., J.L. Belant, B.F. Blackwell, and T.W. Seamans. 2011. Interspecific variation in wildlife hazards to aircraft: implications for airport wildlife management. Wildlife Society Bulletin 35: 394-402.

DeVault, T. L., J. E. Kubel, D. J. Glista, and O. E. Rhodes, Jr. 2008. Mammalian hazards at small airports in Indiana: impact of perimeter fencing. Human-Wildlife Conflicts 2(2):240-247.

Dolbeer, R. A. 2000. Birds and aircraft: fighting for airspace in crowded skies. Pages 37-43 in Proceedings of 19th Vertebrate Pest Conference, University of California, Davis, California, USA.

Dolbeer, R. A. 2006*a*. Birds and aircraft compete for space in crowded skies. ICAO Journal 61(3):21-24. International Civil Aviation Organization. Montreal, Canada.

Dolbeer, R. A. 2006*b*. Height distribution of birds recorded by collisions with aircraft. The Journal of Wildlife Management 70 (5): 1345-1350.

Dolbeer. 2009. Trends in wildlife strike reporting, Part 1—voluntary system, 1990-2008. U.S. Department of Transportation, Federal Aviation Administration, Office of Research and Technology Development, DOT/FAA/AR/09/65. Washington D.C., USA. 20 pages.

Dolbeer, R. A. 2011. Increasing trend of damaging bird strikes with aircraft outside the airport boundary: implications for mitigation measures. Human-Wildlife Interactions 5(2): 31-43.

Dolbeer, R. A., and M. J. Begier. 2012. Comparison of wildlife strike data among airports to improve aviation safety. Proceedings of the 30th International Bird Strike Committee meeting. Stavanger, Norway.

Dolbeer, R. A., M. J. Begier, and S. E. Wright. 2008. Animal ambush: the challenge of managing wildlife hazards at general aviation airports. Proceedings of the 53rd Annual Corporate Aviation Safety Seminar, 30 April-1 May 2008, Palm Harbor, Florida. Flight Safety Foundation, Alexandria, Virginia, USA.

Dolbeer, R. A. and P. Eschenfelder. 2003. Amplified bird-strike risks related to population increases of large birds in North America. Pages 49-67 *in* Proceedings of the 26th International Bird Strike Committee meeting (Volume 1). Warsaw, Poland.

Dolbeer, R. A., J. L. Seubert, and M. J. Begier. 2013. Canada goose populations and strikes with civil aircraft: encouraging trends for the aviation industry. Human-Wildlife Interactions 7 (): In review.

Dolbeer, R. A., and S. E. Wright. 2009. Safety Management Systems: how useful will the FAA National Wildlife Strike Database be? Human-Wildlife Conflicts 3(2):167-178.

Dolbeer, R. A., S. E. Wright, and E. C. Cleary. 1995. Bird and other wildlife strikes to civilian aircraft in the United States, 1994. Interim report, DTFA01-91-Z-02004. U.S. Department of Agriculture, for Federal Aviation Administration, FAA Technical Center, Atlantic City, New Jersey, USA. 38 pages.

Dolbeer, R. A., S. E. Wright, and E. C. Cleary. 2000. Ranking the hazard level of wildlife species to aviation. Wildlife Society Bulletin 28:372–378.

Dolbeer, R. A., S. E. Wright, and P. Eschenfelder. 2005. Animal ambush at the airport: the need to broaden ICAO standards for bird strikes to include terrestrial wildlife.

Pages 102-113 *in* Proceedings of the 27th International Bird Strike Committee meeting (Volume 1). Athens, Greece.

Dove, C.; M. Heacker, F. Dahlan, and J. F. Whatton. 2013. Annual report 2012, birdstrike identification program. Smithsonian Feather Lab, Smithsonian Institution, Washington, D.C., USA. 29 pages.

Dove C. J., N. Rotzel, M. Heacker, and L. A. Weigt. 2008. Using DNA barcodes to identify bird species involved in birdstrikes. Journal of Wildlife Management 72:1231–1236.

Federal Aviation Administration. 2013*a*. Terminal area forecast (TAF) system. Federal Aviation Administration. Washington, D.C., USA (http://aspm.faa.gov/main/taf.asp).

Federal Aviation Administration. 2013*b*. 14 CFR Part 139 certificated airports. Federal Aviation Administration, Washington, D.C., USA. (http://www.faa.gov/airports/airport_safety/part139_cert/media/part139_cert_status_table.xls).

Human Wildlife Conflicts Journal. 2009. Special edition on bird strikes. Volume 3, Issue 2. Berryman Institute, Utah State University, Logan Utah, USA (http://www.berrymaninstitute.org).

Human Wildlife Interactions Journal. 2011. Special edition on bird strikes. Volume 5, Issue 2. Berryman Institute, Utah State University, Logan Utah, USA (http://www.berrymaninstitute.org).

International Civil Aviation Organization. 1989. Manual on the ICAO Bird Strike Information System (IBIS). Third Edition. Montreal, Quebec, Canada.

International Civil Aviation Organization. 1993. Convention on international civil aviation (international standards and recommended practices). Annex 16: Environmental Protection. Third edition. Montreal, Quebec, Canada.

Kelly, T. C., R. Bolger, and M. J. A. O'Callaghan. 1999. The behavioral response of birds to commercial aircraft. Pages 77-82 *in* Bird Strike '99, Proceedings of Bird Strike Committee-USA/Canada Meeting. Vancouver, B.C., Canada: Transport Canada, Ottawa, Ontario, Canada.

Linnell, M.A., M. R. Conover, and T. J. Ohashi. 1999. Biases in bird strike statistics based on pilot reports, The Journal of Wildlife Management 63: 997-1003.

MacKinnon, B., R. Sowden, and S. Dudley, (editors). 2001. Sharing the skies: an aviation guide to the management of wildlife hazards. Transport Canada, Aviation Publishing Division, AARA, 5th Floor, Tower C, 330 Sparks Street, Ottawa, Ontario, K1A 0N8, Canada. 316 pages.

Marra, P. P., C. J. Dove, R. A. Dolbeer, N. F. Dahlan, M. Heacker, J. F. Whatton, N. E. Diggs, C. France, and G. A. Henkes. 2009. Migratory Canada geese cause crash of US Airways Flight 1549. Frontiers in Ecology and the Environment. 7(6): 297-301.

McCabe, T. R., and R. E. McCabe. 1997. Recounting whitetails past. Pages 11–26 *in* W. J. McShea, H. B. Underwood, and J. H. Rappole (editors). The science of overabundance: deer ecology and population management. Smithsonian Institution. Washington D.C., USA. 402 pages.

National Transportation Safety Board. 2010. Loss of thrust in both engines after encountering a flock of birds and subsequent ditching on the Hudson River, US Airways Flight 1549, Airbus A320-214, N106US, Weehawken, New Jersey, January 15, 2009. Aircraft Accident Report NTSB/AAR-10 /03. Washington, D.C., USA.

Richardson, W. J., and T. West. 2000. Serious birdstrike accidents to military aircraft: updated list and summary. Pages 67–98 *in* Proceedings of 25th International Bird Strike Committee Meeting. Amsterdam, Netherlands.

Sauer, J. R., J. E. Hines, J. E. Fallon, K. L. Pardieck, D. J. Ziolkowski, Jr., and W. A. Link. 2012. The North American Breeding Bird Survey, Results and Analysis 1966 - 2011. Version 12.13.2011, U.S. Geologic Survey, Patuxent Wildlife Research Center, Laurel, Maryland, USA.

Thorpe, J. 2003. Fatalities and destroyed aircraft due to bird strikes, 1912–2002. Pages 85–113 *in* Proceedings of the 26th International Bird Strike Committee Meeting (Volume 1). Warsaw, Poland.

Thorpe, J. 2005. Fatalities and destroyed aircraft due to bird strikes, 2002-2004 (with an appendix of animal strikes). Pages 17-24 *in* Proceedings of the 27th International Bird Strike Committee Meeting (Volume 1). Athens, Greece.

Thorpe, J. 2012. 100 years of fatalities and destroyed civil aircraft due to bird strikes. Proceedings of the 30th International Bird Strike Committee Meeting. Stavanger, Norway. (http://www.int-birdstrike.org).

U.S. Department of Transportation. 2013. National Transportation Statistics. Table 1-13: Active U.S. air carrier and general aviation fleet by type of aircraft. Research and Innovative Technology Administration. Washington D.C., USA. (http://www.rita.dot.gov/bts/sites/rita.dot.gov.bts/files/publications/national_transportation_statistics/index.html).

U.S. Fish and Wildlife Service. 2012. Waterfowl population status, 2012. U.S. Department of the Interior, Washington, D.C. USA.

VerCauteren, K. C., C. W. Anderson, T. R. Van Deelen, D. Drake, W. D. Walter, S. M. Vantassel, and S E. Hygnstrom. 2011. Regulated commercial harvest to manage overabundant white-tailed deer: an idea to consider? Wildlife Society Bulletin 35(3):185–194.

Wenning, K. M., M. J. Begier, and R. A. Dolbeer. 2004. Wildlife hazard management at airports: fifteen years of growth and progress for Wildlife Services. Pages 295-301 *in* Proceedings of 21st Vertebrate Pest Conference, University of California, Davis, California, USA.

Wright, S. E. and R. A. Dolbeer. 2005. Percentage of wildlife strikes reported and species identified under a voluntary system. *in* Proceedings of Bird Strike Committee USA/Canada meeting, Vancouver, B.C., Canada (http://www.birdstrikecanada.com).

This page intentionally left blank

TABLES

Table 1. Number of reported wildlife strikes to civil aircraft by wildlife group, USA, 1990–2012 (see Figures 1 and 2).

Year	Birds	Bats	Terrestrial mammals[1]	Reptiles[1]	Total strikes	Strikes with damage
1990	1,795	4	52	0	1,851	372
1991	2,336	3	54	0	2,393	401
1992	2,499	2	73	1	2,575	368
1993	2,504	6	66	0	2,576	399
1994	2,554	2	83	1	2,640	463
1995	2,676	5	84	8	2,773	499
1996	2,853	1	91	3	2,948	505
1997	3,353	1	95	14	3,463	582
1998	3,691	3	111	7	3,812	588
1999	5,022	7	96	1	5,126	706
2000	5,867	16	123	3	6,009	764
2001	5,675	8	138	8	5,829	649
2002	6,102	19	119	15	6,255	674
2003	5,885	20	127	5	6,037	634
2004	6,410	27	129	6	6,572	628
2005	7,092	27	132	7	7,258	609
2006	7,051	49	141	10	7,251	598
2007	7,536	53	172	7	7,768	571
2008	7,417	46	183	5	7,651	530
2009	9,231	67	232	10	9,540	607
2010	9,550	113	246	11	9,920	598
2011	9,770	139	199	15	10,123	541
2012	10,343	164	200	19	10,726	606
Total	**127,212**	**782**	**2,946**	**156**	**131,096**	**12,892**

[1] For terrestrial mammals and reptiles, species with body masses <1 kilogram (2.2 pounds) are excluded from database (Dolbeer et al. 2005).

Table 2. Number and rate of reported wildlife strikes and strikes with damage for commercial air carrier aircraft, USA, 1990–2012 (see Figure 3).

	No. of reported strikes[1]			Strikes/100,000 movements	
Year	All strikes	Strikes with damage	Aircraft movements (x 1 million)[2]	All strikes	Strikes with damage
1990	1,354	215	23.26	5.82	0.92
1991	1,798	251	24.78	7.26	1.01
1992	1,828	212	25.17	7.26	0.84
1993	1,796	229	25.56	7.03	0.90
1994	1,920	282	26.58	7.22	1.06
1995	2,022	321	27.04	7.48	1.19
1996	2,092	313	27.57	7.59	1.14
1997	2,461	364	27.76	8.87	1.31
1998	2,515	361	28.00	8.98	1.29
1999	3,851	475	28.74	13.40	1.65
2000	4,471	510	29.53	15.14	1.73
2001	4,161	442	29.15	14.28	1.52
2002	4,419	462	27.61	16.00	1.67
2003	4,288	417	27.89	15.37	1.50
2004	4,687	402	28.87	16.24	1.39
2005	5,166	416	29.23	17.67	1.42
2006	4,908	404	28.29	17.35	1.43
2007	5,003	354	28.46	17.58	1.24
2008	4,601	337	27.97	16.45	1.21
2009	6,116	386	25.47	24.01	1.52
2010	6,011	377	25.13	23.92	1.50
2011	5,956	338	25.11	23.72	1.35
2012	6,246	381	24.87	25.12	1.53
Total	**87,670**	**8,249**	**597.17**	**14.09**	**1.33**

[1] Strikes involving an unknown operator (28,617 of which 25,651 were "Carcass Found" reports—see Tables 5 and 6) were excluded from this analysis.

[2] Departures and arrivals by air carrier, commuter, and air taxi service (Federal Aviation Administration 2013a).

Table 3. Number and rate of reported wildlife strikes and strikes with damage for general aviation aircraft, USA, 1990–2012 (see Figure 3).

	No. of reported strikes[1]			Strikes/100,000 movements	
Year	All strikes	Strikes with damage	Aircraft movements (x 1 million)[2]	All strikes	Strikes with damage
1990	324	130	77.53	0.42	0.17
1991	401	128	83.52	0.48	0.15
1992	434	144	82.32	0.53	0.17
1993	445	158	80.39	0.55	0.20
1994	477	175	79.18	0.60	0.22
1995	482	168	77.20	0.62	0.22
1996	509	181	79.00	0.64	0.23
1997	506	189	79.98	0.63	0.24
1998	578	207	84.28	0.69	0.25
1999	624	213	85.38	0.73	0.25
2000	684	248	87.13	0.79	0.28
2001	701	198	85.95	0.82	0.23
2002	793	210	85.81	0.92	0.24
2003	695	211	83.48	0.83	0.25
2004	711	222	82.72	0.86	0.27
2005	677	192	81.18	0.83	0.24
2006	694	194	80.20	0.87	0.24
2007	679	214	80.27	0.85	0.27
2008	670	191	78.11	0.86	0.24
2009	886	220	73.69	1.20	0.30
2010	863	218	71.32	1.21	0.31
2011	938	203	69.99	1.34	0.29
2012	1,038	225	70.12	1.48	0.32
Total	**14,809**	**4,439**	**1,768.63**	**0.81**	**0.24**

[1] Strikes involving an unknown operator (28,617 of which 25,651 were "Carcass Found" reports—see Tables 5 and 6) were excluded from this analysis.

[2] Itinerant and local departures and arrivals by GA aircraft (Federal Aviation Administration 2013a).

Table 4. Source of information for reported wildlife strikes to civil aircraft, USA, 1990–2012 and 2012 only.

Source	1990–2012		2012 only	
	Total	% of total	Total	% of total
FAA Form 5200-7E[1] (Electronic)	53,335	41	9,245	86
FAA Form 5200-7[1] (Paper)	41,526	32	453	4
Airline report	14,444	11	252	2
Multiple[2]	10,314	8	471	4
Airport report	5,969	5	133	1
Other[3]	1,739	1	54	1
Daily Report (FAA)	886	1	114	1
Preliminary Aircraft Incident Report	983	1	0	0
Engine manufacturer	822	1	0	0
Aircraft Incident Report	711	1	0	0
Aviation Safety Reporting System	197	<1	0	0
National Transportation Safety Board	81	<1	1	0
Aircraft Incident Preliminary Notice	67	<1	1	<1
Transport Canada	22	<1	2	<1
Total	131,096	100	10,726	100

[1] Bird/Other Wildlife Strike Report. Electronic filing of reports (http://wildlife.faa.gov) began in April 2001. In 2001, 0.4 percent of reports were filed electronically compared to 20, 28, 32, 38, 46, 62, 67, 71, 78, 84 and 86 percent in 2002–2012, respectively. The paper version of FAA Form 5200-7 (mailed to FAA headquarters) declined from 57 percent of all reports in 2001 to 21 percent in 2006 and only 4 percent in 2012.

[2] More than one type of report was filed for the same strike.

[3] Various sources such as news media and Commercial Incident Reports.

Table 5. Person filing report of wildlife strike to civil aircraft, USA, 1990–2012 and 2012 only.

Person filing report	1990–2012		2012 only	
	Total	% of total	Total	% of total
Carcass Found	26,733	24	3,381	33
Airline Operations	26,458	24	1,103	11
Pilot	25,651	23	2,289	23
Airport Operations	17,830	16	2,718	27
Tower	11,215	10	425	4
Other	2,865	3	203	2
Total known	**110,752**	**100**	**10,119**	**100**
Unknown	**20,344**		**607**	
Total	**131,096**		**10,726**	

[1] Airport personnel found fresh wildlife remains within 250 feet of a runway centerline that appeared to have been struck by aircraft, but no strike was observed or reported by pilot, tower, or airline.

Table 6. Number of reported wildlife strikes to civil aircraft by type of operator, USA, 1990–2012 and 2012 only.

Type of operator	1990–2012		2012 only	
	Total	% of total	Total	% of total
Commercial[1]	**87,670**	**86**	**6,246**	**86**
General aviation	**14,809**	**14**	**1,038**	**14**
Business	11,493	11	863	12
Private	2,276	2	71	1
Government/ Police[2]	1,040	1	104	1
Total known	**102,479**	**100**	**7,284**	**100**
Unknown[3]	**28,617**		**3,442**	
Total	**131,096**		**10,726**	

[1] Air carrier, commuter, and air taxi service with 3-letter Operator Code.

[2] U.S. Customs and Border Protection and U.S. Coast Guard aircraft were respectively involved in 32 percent (330) and 25 percent (256) of the 1,040 Government/police strikes.

[3] Ninety percent (25,651) of the 28,617 strikes involving an unknown operator were "Carcass Found" reports (see Table 5).

Table 7. Number of Part 139-certificated airports[1] and General Aviation (GA) airports with reported wildlife strikes and number of strikes reported, civil aircraft, 1990–2012 (see also Figure 5)[2].

Year	Part 139 airports		GA airports		All USA airports	
	Airports	Strikes	Airports	Strikes	Airports	Strikes
1990	236	1,507	96	165	332	1,672
1991	259	1,982	97	209	356	2,191
1992	255	2,189	108	233	363	2,422
1993	258	2,219	98	222	356	2,441
1994	266	2,230	109	250	375	2,480
1995	261	2,323	119	225	380	2,548
1996	259	2,502	110	206	369	2,708
1997	284	2,905	123	213	407	3,118
1998	293	3,226	143	273	436	3,499
1999	302	3,816	148	269	450	4,085
2000	313	4,467	151	288	464	4,755
2001	317	4,438	150	302	467	4,740
2002	306	4,789	157	319	463	5,108
2003	305	4,683	152	346	457	5,029
2004	309	5,216	175	326	484	5,542
2005	321	5,518	176	341	497	5,859
2006	322	5,927	143	281	465	6,208
2007	328	6,572	166	340	494	6,912
2008	330	6,642	165	316	495	6,958
2009	366	8,040	231	459	597	8,499
2010	376	8,305	213	470	589	8,775
2011	368	8,451	228	505	596	8,956
2012	387	8,760	256	585	643	9,345
Total	**531**	**106,707**	**1,240**	**7,143**	**1,771**	**113,850**

[1] There are about 550 airports in USA certificated for passenger service under CFR Part 139 regulations (FAA 2013b).

[2] In addition, 2,864 strikes involving USA-registered aircraft were reported from 273 foreign airports. Furthermore, 14,382 strikes were reported in which aircraft was en route when strike occurred (Table 10), evidence of strike was discovered on aircraft after landing but phase of flight where strike occurred could not be determined, or airport was not named on reporting form.

Table 8. Reported time of occurrence of wildlife strikes with civil aircraft, USA, 1990–2012[1].

Time of day	Birds		Terrestrial mammals	
	23-year total	% of total known	23-year total	% of total known
Dawn	3,038	4	51	3
Day	51,403	62	425	25
Dusk	3,805	5	142	8
Night	24,019	29	1,066	63
Total known	**82,265**	**100**	**1,684**	**100**
Unknown[2]	**44,947**		**1,262**	
Total	**127,212**		**2,946**	

[1] In addition, 782 strikes with bats were reported from 1990–2012: time not reported (566), night (173), dusk (13), day (27), and dawn (3). Also, 156 strikes with reptiles were reported from 1990–2012: time not reported (132), day (16), night (5), dusk (2), and dawn (1).

[2] Unknowns include 25,651 "Carcass Found" reports (Table 5).

Table 9. Reported phase of flight at time of occurrence of wildlife strikes with civil aircraft, USA, 1990–2012[1].

Phase of flight	Birds 23-year total	Birds % of total known	Terrestrial mammals 23-year total	Terrestrial mammals % of total known
Parked	61	0	2	0
Taxi	304	0	40	2
Take-off Run	16,456	19	583	32
Climb	15,562	18	39	2
En Route	2,299	3	0	0
Descent	2,931	3	0	0
Approach	35,722	40	1,038	57
Landing Roll	15,019	17	131	7
Total known	**88,354**	**100**	**1,833**	**100**
Unknown	**38,858**		**1,113**	
Total	**127,212**		**2,946**	

[1] In addition, 782 strikes with bats were reported from 1990–2012: phase of flight not reported (569), approach (149), landing roll (23), climb (22), descent (5), take-off run (8), and en route (6). Also, 156 strikes with reptiles were reported: phase of flight not reported (122), take-off run (12), taxi (7), approach (5; pilot had a missed approach because reptile was on the runway), and landing roll (10).

[2] Terrestrial mammal (e.g., deer, coyote) was hit after aircraft had lifted off runway or just before touchdown, or pilot had a missed approach because terrestrial mammal was on the runway.

Table 10. Number of reported bird strikes to commercial civil aircraft[1] by height above ground level (AGL), USA, 1990–2012. See Figures 7 and 8 for graphic analysis of strike data from 501 to 18,500 feet AGL[2].

Height of strike (feet AGL)	All reported strikes			Strikes with damage		
	23-year total	% of total known	% cum- ulative total	23-year total	% of total known	% cum- ulative total
0	26,773	41	41	1,651	29	29
1-500	20,154	31	72	1,583	28	57
501-1500	7,014	11	82	833	15	72
1501-2500	3,591	6	88	505	9	80
2501-3500	2,660	4	92	315	6	86
3501-4500	1,578	2	94	186	3	89
4501-5500	1,153	2	96	151	3	92
5501-6500	772	1	97	114	2	94
6501-7500	530	1	98	76	1	95
7501-8500	394	1	99	69	1	97
8501-9500	214	<1	99	30	<1	97
9501-10500	281	<1	99	49	<1	98
10501-11500	149	<1	>99	39	<1	99
>11500[3]	249	<1	100	80	<1	100
Total known	**65,512**	**100**		**5,681**	**100**	
Unknown height	**21,369**			**2,411**		
Total	**86,881**			**8,092**		

[1] Air carrier, commuter, and air taxi service with 3-letter Operator Code (see Table 6); 1,100 strikes in which height of strike was reported but type of operator was unknown were excluded from analysis.

[2] A more detailed analysis of bird strikes by height AGL is provided by Dolbeer (2006b).

[3] Twenty-one strikes involving commercial aircraft (8 with damage to aircraft) were reported at ≥20,000 feet AGL; the highest was 31,300 feet.

Table 11. Number of reported bird strikes to general aviation aircraft[1] by height above ground level (AGL), USA, 1990–2012. See Figures 7 and 8 for graphic analysis of strike data from 501 to 18,500 feet AGL[2].

Height of strike (feet AGL)	All reported strikes			Strikes with damage		
	23-year total	% of total known	% cumulative total	23-year total	% of total known	% cumulative total
0	4,502	37	37	561	18	18
1-500	4,450	37	74	1,095	34	52
501-1500	1,679	14	88	805	25	77
1501-2500	698	6	94	280	9	86
2501-3500	314	3	97	222	7	93
3501-4500	118	1	98	88	3	96
4501-5500	122	1	99	48	2	97
5501-6500	49	<1	99	29	1	98
6501-7500	41	<1	99	22	1	99
7501-8500	15	<1	>99	9	0	99
8501-9500	15	<1	>99	9	0	99
9501-10500	12	<1	>99	7	0	99
10,501-11500	4	<1	>99	3	0	100
>11500[3]	18	<1	100	13	0	100
Total known	**12,037**	**100**		**3,191**	**100**	
Unknown height	**1,419**			**416**		
Total	**13,456**			**3,607**		

[1] Private, Business, and Government/Police aircraft (see Table 6); 1,100 strikes in which height of strike was reported but type of operator was unknown were excluded from analysis.

[2] A more detailed analysis of bird strikes by height AGL is provided by Dolbeer (2006b).

[3] Three strikes involving general aviation aircraft (all with damage to aircraft) were reported at $\geq$20,000 feet AGL; the highest was 24,000 feet.

Table 12. Civil aircraft components reported as being struck and damaged by wildlife, USA, 1990–2012.

Aircraft component	Birds (23-year total)				Terrestrial mammals (23-year total)			
	Number struck	% of total	Number damaged	% of total	Number struck	% of total	Number damaged	% of total
Windshield	18,958	17	879	6	7	0	15	1
Engine(s)[1]	15,013	13	4,206	30	173	7	173	9
Nose	16,355	14	876	6	95	4	94	5
Wing/rotor	15,323	13	3,288	23	270	11	283	15
Radome	14,263	13	1,377	10	14	1	15	1
Fuselage	14,080	12	577	4	130	5	140	8
Other	10,034	9	1,080	8	315	13	270	15
Landing gear	5,112	4	458	3	1,019	42	434	24
Propeller	2,638	2	242	2	300	12	284	15
Tail	1,501	1	566	4	60	2	80	4
Light	784	1	588	4	40	2	46	3
Total[2]	**114,061**	**100**	**14,137**	**100**	**2,423**	**100**	**1,834**	**100**

[1] For birds, 15,013 engines were reported as struck in 14,322 strike events involving engines (13,656 events with one engine struck, 647 with two engines struck, 13 with three engines struck, and 6 with four engines struck). A total of 4,206 engines was damaged in 4,069 bird-strike events with engine damage (3,935 events with one engine damaged, 132 with two engines damaged, 1 with three engines damaged, and 1 with 4 engines damaged). For terrestrial mammals, 173 engines were reported as struck in 163 strike events (153 events with one engine struck and 10 with two engines struck). A total of 173 engines was damaged in 154 terrestrial mammal strike events with engine damage (135 events with one engine damaged and 19 with two engines damaged). Some engines were damaged without being struck when the landing gear collapsed.

[2] In addition, bat strikes had 333 and 11 components reported as struck and damaged, respectively: radome/nose (110, 1), windshield (63, 2), engine (28, 3), propeller (1, 0), wing/rotor (55, 4), fuselage (30, 0), tail (8, 0), other (22, 0), landing gear (14, 0), light (2, 1). For reptile strikes, there were 29 and 6 components reported struck and damaged, respectively: windshield (1, 1), wing/rotor (1, 1), fuselage (1, 1), landing gear (24, 1); tail (1, 1), other (1, 1).

Table 13. Number of civil aircraft with reported damage resulting from wildlife strikes, USA, 1990–2012. See Tables 1, 2 and 3 and Figures 2, 3, 4 and 9 for trends in damaging strikes from 1990–2012.

| Damage category[2] | Reported strikes | | | | | |
| | Birds | | Terrestrial mammals | | Total[1] | |
	23-year total	% of total[3]	23-year total	% of total[3]	23-year total	% of total[3]
None	**82,189**	**65**	**757**	**26**	**83,243**	**63**
Unknown	**33,142**	**26**	**1,192**	**40**	**34,963**	**27**
Damage	**11,881**	**9**	**997**	**34**	**12,890**	**10**
Minor	6,403	5	516	18	6,926	5
Uncertain	2,443	2	67	2	2,511	2
Substantial	3,003	2	386	13	3,393	3
Destroyed	32	<1	28	1	60	<1
Total	**127,212**	**100**	**2,946**	**100**	**131,096**	**100**

[1] Included in totals are 782 and 156 strikes involving bats and reptiles, respectively. For bats, 274 reports indicated no damage, 498 failed to report if damage occurred, and 10 reported damage (6 minor, 1 uncertain level, 3 substantial). For reptiles, 23 reports indicated no damage, 131 failed to report if damage occurred, and 2 reported damage (1 minor, 1 substantial).

[2] The damage codes and descriptions are from the International Civil Aviation Organization (1989): Minor = the aircraft can be rendered airworthy by simple repairs or replacements and an extensive inspection is not necessary; Uncertain = the aircraft was damaged, but details as to the extent of the damage are lacking; Substantial = the aircraft incurs damage or structural failure that adversely affects the structure strength, performance, or flight characteristics of the aircraft and that would normally require major repair or replacement of the affected component (specifically excluded are bent fairings or cowlings; small dents or puncture holes in the skin; damage to wing tips, antenna, tires, or brakes; and engine blade damage not requiring blade replacement); Destroyed = the damage sustained makes it inadvisable to restore the aircraft to an airworthy condition.

[3] The percentage of strikes causing damage is calculated using the total strikes reported as the divisor, including the 34,963 reports that did not indicate if damage occurred or not (Unknown). "Carcass found" reports (see Table 5) comprised 25,651 (73 percent) of these 34,963 reports. If the Unknown reports are excluded from the calculations, then 13, 57, and 13 percent of the strikes caused damage for birds, terrestrial mammals, and all species, respectively.

Table 14. Reported effect-on-flight (EOF) of wildlife strikes to civil aircraft, USA, 1990–2012.

| Effect-on-flight[2] | Reported strikes | | | | | |
| | Birds | | Terrestrial mammals | | Total[1] | |
	23-year total	% of total	23-year total	% of total	23-year total	% of total
None	**68,546**	**54**	**698**	**24**	**69,518**	**53**
Unknown	**50,277**	**40**	**1,585**	**54**	**52,510**	**40**
Negative effect	**8,389**	**7**	**663**	**23**	**9,068**	**7**
Precautionary landing	4,538	4	99	3	4,644	4
Aborted takeoff	1,778	1	212	7	1,990	2
Engine shutdown	372	<1	29	1	401	<1
Other	1,701	1	323	11	2,033	2
Total	**127,212**	**100**	**2,946**	**100**	**131,096**	**100**

[1] Included in totals are 782 and 156 strikes involving bats and reptiles, respectively. For bats, 248 reports indicated no effect-on-flight, 526 failed to report if an effect-on-flight occurred, and 8 reported a negative effect (6 precautionary landings, 2 "Other"). For reptiles, 26 reports indicated no effect-on-flight, 122 failed to report if an effect-on-flight occurred, and 8 reported a negative effect (1 precautionary landing, 7 "Other").

[2] Effect-on-flight: None = flight continued as scheduled, although delays and other cost caused by inspections or repairs may have been incurred after landing; Aborted take-off = pilot aborted take-off on departure runway after initiating takeoff run (aircraft may have become airborne but pilot landed on departing runway without doing a "go around"); Precautionary landing (includes "declared emergency" landings) = pilot completed take-off but returned to land at departure airport or landed at an "other-than-destination" airport after strike; Engine shut down = pilot shut down engine or engine stopped running because of strike; Other = miscellaneous effects, such as reduced speed because of shattered windshield, flight delays, or crash landing; Unknown = report did not give sufficient information to determine an effect-on-flight (Dolbeer et al. 2000).

[3] The percentage of strikes causing negative effect-on-flight is calculated using the total strikes reported as the divisor, including the 50,277 reports that did not indicate if a negative effect occurred or not (Unknown). "Carcass found" reports (see Table 5) comprised 25,651 (51 percent) of these 50,277 reports. If the Unknown reports are excluded from the calculations, then 11, 49, and 12 percent of the strikes caused a negative effect-on-flight for birds, terrestrial mammals, and all species, respectively.

Table 15. Number of reported incidents where pilot made a precautionary or emergency landing after striking birds during departure in which fuel was jettisoned or burned (circling pattern) to lighten aircraft weight or in which an overweight (greater than maximum landing weight) landing was made (no fuel jettison or burn), USA civil aircraft, 1990–2012. See Figure 10 for trend in incidents, 1990–2012.

Action taken after bird strike on departure	Number of incidents	Comments and number of incidents by aircraft model
Fuel jettison	45	A mean of 90,306 lbs (13,280 gallons) of fuel jettisoned per incident (range 3,500 – 270,000 lbs; 515 - 39,706 gallons). Aircraft: B-747 (17), B-767 (7), B-727 (6), DC-10/MD-11 (8), B-777 (2), Learjet 31/35 (2), L-1011 (1), DA-2000 (1), unknown (1).
Fuel burn	46	Aircraft: CL-RJ 100/700/900 (7), EMB-120/145/170 (7), A-319/320/321 (5), B-737 (4); MD-80/88 (2); B-747, DHC8-Dash 8, and PA-28 (2 each); and 15 other aircraft types with 1 each.
Overweight landing	80	Aircraft: B-737 (22), A-320/330 (14), B-757 (14), MD-80/82 (9), B-767 (8), EMB-145/170 (3), A-300, MD-11, and C-500/600 (2 each), and CL-RJ 900, CRJ-400, DA-50 Falcon, and Dornier 328 (1 each).
Total	171	A mean of 7.4 (range 0 – 16) incidents (fuel jettison, fuel burn, or overweight landing) per year, 1990 – 2012.

Table 16. Aircraft speed (nautical miles/hour [knots])[1] at time pilot aborted takeoff after striking or observing a bird or other wildlife species on runway, civil aircraft, USA, 1990–2012. See Figure 11 for trend in aborted take-offs at $\geq$80 knots caused by birds or other wildlife, 1990–2012.

Aircraft speed (knots)	Commercial aircraft[2]		General aviation aircraft[3]		All aircraft[4]	
	23-year total	% of total known	23-year total	% of total known	23-year total	% of total known
1-39	15	2	22	5	38	3
40-79	125	17	209	47	338	28
80-119	503	67	187	42	695	57
$\geq$120	112	15	27	6	141	12
Total known	**755**	**100**	**445**	**100**	**1,212**	**100**
Unknown	**508**		**252**		**784**	
Total	**1,263**		**697**		**1,996**[5]	

[1] A speed of 100 knots equals 185 kilometers/hour (115 miles/hour).

[2] Air carrier, commuter, and air taxi service with 3-letter identifying code (see Table 6).

[3.] Business, Private, or Government aircraft (see Table 6).

[4] Included in totals are 36 aborted takeoffs in which type of operator was unknown. For these 36 events, the speed was unreported (24), 1-39 knots (1), 40-79 knots (4), 80-119 knots (5), and $\geq$120 knots (2).

[5] Includes 6 incidents in which effect-on-flight was classified as "Engine shutdown" (Table 14) but pilot also aborted take-off.

Table 17. Total reported strikes, strikes causing damage, strikes having a negative effect-on-flight (EOF), strikes involving >1 animal, aircraft downtime, and costs by identified wildlife species for civil aircraft, USA, 1990–2012 (page 1 of 20).

Wildlife group or species	23-year totals (1990–2012)					
	Number of reported strikes				Reported economic losses[1]	
	Total	With dam-age	With neg. EOF	With multiple animals[2]	Aircraft down time (hrs)	Reported costs ($)
Birds						
Loons	**34**	**21**	**16**		**3,271**	**3,039,679**
Loons	2	1	1			
Common loon	27	17	12		2,861	3,020,678
Red-throated loon	4	2	3		218	17,683
Pacific loon	1	1			192	1,318
Grebes	**70**	**16**	**10**	**10**	**1,614**	**3,029,746**
Grebes	11	2	1	1	1,440	522,850
Eared grebe	6	1		1	10	144,633
Western grebe	18	8	6	6	90	2,226,181
Pied-billed grebe	21	1	1			
Horned grebe	9	3	1	1	74	136,082
Red-necked grebe	3	1	1	1		
Clark's grebe	1					
Great crested grebe	1					
Albatroses/shearwaters	**70**	**8**	**6**	**2**	**197**	**78,082**
Laysan albatross	35	7	5	1	197	78,082
Black-footed albatross	5	1				
Bonin petrel	8			1		
Wedge-tailed shearwater	10		1			
Townsend's shearwater	11					
Fork-tailed storm-petrel	1					
Tropicbirds	**20**	**11**	**10**		**204**	**108,519**
Tropicbirds	10	7	5		148	61,092
White-tailed tropicbird	7	3	4		56	39,743
Red-tailed tropicbird	3	1	1			7,684
Pelicans	**76**	**38**	**32**	**14**	**4,856**	**10,303,646**
Pelicans	3	2			80	
Australian pelican	1	1	1			
Brown pelican	59	25	21	8	496	462,548
American white pelican	13	10	10	6	4,280	9,841,098
Red-footed booby	**1**					
Cormorants	**106**	**36**	**25**	**17**	**594**	**3,817,231**
Cormorants	2					
Great cormorant	2	1		2		
Double-crstd cormorant	100	34	24	15	570	3,817,231

Table 17. Continued (Page 2 of 20)

Wildlife group or species	23-year totals (1990–2012)					
	Number of reported strikes				Reported economic losses[1]	
	Total	With damage	With neg. EOF	With multiple animals[2]	Aircraft down time (hrs)	Reported costs ($)
Pelagic cormorant	1					
Brandt's cormorant	1	1	1		24	
Anhinga	**25**	**12**	**9**	**4**	**167**	**273,667**
Frigatebirds	**15**	**6**	**2**		**22**	**23,707**
Frigatebirds	5	3	1		19	16,236
Great frigatebird	8	2	1		3	7,471
Magnificent frigatebird	2	1				
Herons/bitterns	**510**	**90**	**67**	**18**	**4,510**	**6,824,063**
Herons	52	13	10	4	99	4,250
Gray heron	1	1	1			
Great blue heron	305	65	50	8	3,698	6,425,605
Blk-crowned night-heron	57	4	2	2	49	320,568
Little blue heron	7					
Green heron	13			1		
Ylw-crowned night-heron	16	4	2	1	18	19,395
Tricolored heron	2					
American bittern	7	3	2		646	54,245
Yellow bittern	49			2		
Least bittern	1					
Egrets	**676**	**73**	**100**	**154**	**4,056**	**7,006,666**
Egrets	316	32	50	84	3,609	4,501,202
Cattle egret	269	27	41	59	239	76,740
Great egret	62	11	8	10	158	2,428,724
Intermediate egret	1					
Snowy egret	28	3	1	1	50	
Storks	**14**	**5**	**2**	**3**	**24**	**22,224**
White stork	1	1				
Wood stork	13	4	2	3	24	22,224
Ibises/spoonbills	**30**	**11**	**11**	**8**	**148**	**59,782**
Ibises	5		1	1		
Glossy ibis	2	1	1	1		2,053
White ibis	10	3	4	1	132	57,729
White-faced ibis	11	7	4	5	15	
Roseate spoonbill	2		1		1	
Waterfowl	**4,137**	**1,767**	**900**	**1,477**	**144,552**	**212,881,798**
Ducks, geese, swans	137	65	31	55	763	1,212,121
Ducks	764	267	127	250	8,945	6,094,707
American wigeon	51	23	8	16	5,056	1,929,314

Table 17. Continued (Page 3 of 20)

Wildlife group or species	23-year totals (1990–2012)					
	Number of reported strikes				Reported economic losses[1]	
	Total	With dam-age	With neg. EOF	With multiple animals[2]	Aircraft down time (hrs)	Reported costs ($)
Northern pintail	116	59	35	56	1,896	2,362,915
Green-winged teal	46	14	7	15	774	888,374
Blue-winged teal	23	11	6	8	217	827,010
Eurasian wigeon	1			1		
Mallard	688	158	86	159	10,325	15,466,912
Common eider	3	2	1	1		
Ring-necked duck	17	6	3	5	1,116	90,443
Greater scaup	8	3	3	4		
Wood duck	39	13	6	8	468	120,232
Muscovy duck	1	1			120	592,454
Common goldeneye	5	2	1			2,405
Red-breasted merganser	4	1		1	2	
Hooded merganser	7	3		1	54	253,851
Common merganser	3	2	2	1	120	3,712
Northern shoveler	53	23	7	18	2,233	2,190,055
Gadwall	48	19	8	14	614	8,280,430
Canvasback	17	9	4	6	575	2,584,009
American black duck	41	4	2	13	2,388	72,153
Mottled duck	22	4	4	5	25	
Lesser scaup	34	17	11	10	1,479	259,285
Ruddy duck	38	11	3	5	100	94,895
Redhead	4	2		2	17	54,114
Bufflehead	8	1	2	1	40	5,416
Long-tailed duck	4	3	3	1	3	1,222
Philippine duck	1	1	1	1	96	11,675,885
Blk-bellied whistling-duck	3	1	1	1	48	
Cinnamon teal	4	1		1	20	6,653
White-winged scoter	1	1	1	1	1,400	503,681
Hawaiian duck	11			3		
Harlequin duck	1					
Barrow's goldeneye	1					
Geese	333	203	90	116	25,607	2,890,868
Snow goose	109	84	43	63	10,288	30,794,155
Canada goose	1,400	701	385	596	68,301	116,295,969
Brant	27	10	3	7	108	59,087
Grtr white-fronted goose	37	24	8	21	759	5,525,841
Emperor goose	2	1				
Cackling goose	3	3		2	101	132,581

Table 17. Continued (Page 4 of 20)

Wildlife group or species	23-year totals (1990–2012)					
	Number of reported strikes				Reported economic losses[1]	
	Total	With damage	With neg. EOF	With multiple animals[2]	Aircraft down time (hrs)	Reported costs ($)
Swans	2	1				
Mute swan	8	2	1	2		
Tundra swan	10	9	5	6	422	470,127
Trumpeter swan	2	2	2	1	72	1,140,922
Hawks, eagles, vultures	**4,590**	**1,141**	**758**	**161**	**101,464**	**89,719,231**
Hawks, eagles, vultures	30	17	7	1	2,559	23,461
New World Vultures	289	168	85	26	25,469	11,747,177
Black vulture	93	59	38	8	5,595	4,701,233
Turkey vulture	487	250	170	29	29,066	10,000,834
Osprey	240	53	35	4	2,597	401,808
White-tailed kite	26	4	2		46	6,013,185
Black kite	2	1	1			
Mississippi kite	1					
Swallow-tailed kite	3		1		1	36
Eagles	6	3	2	1		
Bald eagle	155	63	43	11	6,893	24,060,519
White-bellied sea-eagle	1	1	1			
Golden eagle	13	2	3	1	3,696	938,488
Hawks	1,195	239	165	31	11,867	5,377,922
Northern goshawk	2					
Red-tailed hawk	1,659	249	182	40	11,108	15,707,275
Rough-legged hawk	64	5	3		1	43,488
Red-shouldered hawk	31	2	4		42	1,519
Swainson's hawk	78	10	7	2	981	444,757
Sharp-shinned hawk	19	1			1,000	379,488
Cooper's hawk	56	3	3	2	3	
Ferruginous hawk	15	2	1		26	3,651,019
Broad-winged hawk	13	3	2	1	250	5,411
Harris's hawk	2					
White-tailed hawk	2					
Eurasian buzzard	2	1			24	
Northern harrier	102	2	2	3		281,742
Old world vultures	3	2		1		
Lappet-faced vulture	1	1	1		240	5,939,869
Falcons and Caracaras	**3,595**	**48**	**77**	**157**	**1,648**	**3,035,861**
Falcons	44	3	3	2	82	55,118
Peregrine falcon	224	17	12	9	187	544,973

Table 17. Continued (Page 5 of 20)

Wildlife group or species	23-year totals (1990–2012)					
	Number of reported strikes				Reported economic losses[1]	
	Total	With damage	With neg. EOF	With multiple animals[2]	Aircraft down time (hrs)	Reported costs ($)
Gyrfalcon	2					
Merlin	58	1	3	3	23	514,089
Crested caracara	7	1	1			
Prairie falcon	19	1	1	2		5,953
American kestrel	3,236	24	56	141	1,356	1,915,728
Eurasian kestrel	5	1	1			
Gallinaceous birds	**228**	**62**	**47**	**48**	**2,504**	**1,092,395**
Grouse	6	2		3	2	
Greater sage-grouse	33	12	6	13	554	494,188
Sharp-tailed grouse	5	1	1		24	783
Ruffed grouse	1					
Ptarmigans	3	1	1	2	18	70,435
Willow ptarmigan	6	3	1	4	207	134,052
Rock ptarmigan	1	1				
Quails	9		3	2		
Northern bobwhite	9	2	3	1	73	1,127
Scaled quail	3					
Ring-necked pheasant	75	17	13	5	883	107,750
Red-legged partridge	1					
Gray partridge	9	3	3	4	28	209
Chukar	2		1	1		
Gray francolin	3					
Black francolin	4					
Helmeted guineafowl	1	1		1		
Wild turkey	57	19	15	12	715	283,851
Cranes	**112**	**46**	**30**	**34**	**2,411**	**282,776**
Sandhill crane	111	45	30	34	2,363	223,857
Whooping crane	1	1			48	58,919
Rails/gallinules	**193**	**39**	**20**	**9**	**3,201**	**6,983,256**
Rails	5	1	1	1		
Sora	21	1	1	1	68	19,501
Common moorhen	4	1	1		24	1,255
American coot	147	35	16	7	3,034	6,932,689
Eurasian coot	1					
Purple gallinule	4	1	1		72	29,811
Virginia rail	6				3	
Clapper rail	5					

Table 17. Continued (Page 6 of 20)

Wildlife group or species	23-year totals (1990–2012)					
	Number of reported strikes				Reported economic losses[1]	
	Total	With damage	With neg. EOF	With multiple animals[2]	Aircraft down time (hrs)	Reported costs ($)
Shorebirds	**4,985**	**111**	**142**	**772**	**2,417**	**5,445,938**
Shorebirds	21			9		
American oystercatcher	22			2		
Plovers, lapwings	1			1		
Plovers	48	3	4	8	24	
European golden-plover	5					
American golden-plover	108	4	4	31	9	1,171
Black-bellied plover	97	6	5	18	27	198,486
Snowy plover	1			1		
Killdeer	2,920	41	54	306	745	3,990,279
Pacific golden-plover	753	6	10	107	136	326,756
Semipalmated plover	57			18		
Piping plover	1	1		1	2	216
Wilson's plover	3					
Northern lapwing	1	1	1	1	25	
Southern lapwing	1	1	1			10,413
Sandpipers, curlews	228	14	25	80	179	202,544
Upland sandpiper	164	6	6	16	16	2,539
Spotted sandpiper	19	2	1	3		
Willet	6			2		
Common snipe	5			1		
American woodcock	51	2	2	3	20	11,573
Dunlin	42	3	3	13	507	253,608
Baird's sandpiper	17			1		
Western sandpiper	70	4	5	50	97	143,184
Pectoral sandpiper	15	1	1	4		351
Sanderling	22	1	3	9	6	
Buff-breasted sandpiper	26			7		
Ruddy turnstone	15			1		
Least sandpiper	78	1	5	27	8	
Semipalmated sandpiper	41		1	20	1	
Lesser yellowlegs	9	1		2		
Short-billed dowitcher	6	2		2	6	10,267
Hudsonian godwit	5	1	1	2	96	33,982
Solitary sandpiper	3			1		
Greater yellowlegs	3	1			48	8,890
Long-billed dowitcher	9			4	1	
Red knot	4		1			

Table 17. Continued (Page 7 of 20)

Wildlife group or species	23-year totals (1990–2012)					
	Number of reported strikes				Reported economic losses[1]	
	Total	With dam-age	With neg. EOF	With multiple animals[2]	Aircraft down time (hrs)	Reported costs ($)
White-rumped sandpiper	7			1		
Black turnstone	1					
Marbled godwit	2	1	1	1	48	168,751
Wilson's snipe	54	3	3	4	20	17,490
Rock sandpiper	1			1		
Eurasian curlew	1					
Whimbrel	15	2	1	3	360	52,707
Long-billed curlew	5			1		
Red-necked phalarope	4	1	1	1		
Wilson's phalarope	6	1	3	3	36	12,731
Red phalarope	1					
American avocet	5	1		3		
Black-necked stilt	5			3		
Double-striped thick-knee	1					
Gulls/jaegers	**9,252**	**1,321**	**1,095**	**2,021**	**56,961**	**52,697,794**
Parasitic jaeger	2					
Long-tailed jaeger	2					
Gulls	6,116	1,036	836	1,550	41,457	27,772,584
Herring gull	996	97	91	105	2,072	2,816,792
Mew gull	57	6	4	8	28	101,296
Ring-billed gull	1,193	99	89	218	6,053	4,258,912
Glaucous-winged gull	89	19	11	14	298	1,762,671
Great black-backed gull	95	10	6	9	121	434,817
Franklin's gull	85	4	8	30	20	176,427
Laughing gull	337	18	22	46	731	711,528
Bonaparte's gull	32	2	3	9		91,566
Lesser black-backed gull	5	2	1	1		
Western gull	100	11	7	11	203	1,971,421
California gull	115	13	12	13	5,022	680,086
Heermann's gull	1			1		
Black-headed gull	5					
Thayer's gull	3					
Yellow-legged gull	3	3	3	3	456	11,603,454
Glaucous gull	16	1	2	3	500	316,240
Terns/kittiwakes	**151**	**5**	**3**	**28**	**4**	**77,059**
Terns	41	2		13		
Little tern	1					
Caspian tern	19			1		

Table 17. Continued (Page 8 of 20)

Wildlife group or species	23-year totals (1990–2012)					
	Number of reported strikes				Reported economic losses[1]	
	Total	With dam-age	With neg. EOF	With multiple animals[2]	Aircraft down time (hrs)	Reported costs ($)
Common tern	16	1		3		77,059
Sandwich tern	1					
Gull-billed tern	4					
Black tern	1					
Fairy tern	3					
White tern	4		1	1		
Arctic tern	4	1		2		
Roseate tern	1					
Forster's tern	10		1	2	4	
Least tern	19			2		
Black noddy	3			2		
Brown noddy	7		1	1		
Royal tern	3					
Sooty tern	3					
Black-legged kittiwake	2					
Red-legged kittiwake	1					
Black skimmer	8	1		1		
Pigeons, doves	**9,141**	**440**	**533**	**1,990**	**25,894**	**20,588,663**
Pigeons, doves	21	2	3	12	36	660
Pigeons	14	1	1	5	6	
Common wood-pigeon	4			1		
Band-tailed pigeon	9	4		3	179	188,858
Rock pigeon	2,333	229	224	789	14,280	11,331,342
Doves	897	43	73	212	617	631,006
Eurasian collared-dove	3					
Mourning dove	5,362	151	221	932	10,516	8,085,982
Spotted dove	174	4	6	10	133	347,679
Zebra dove	263	3	5	24	25	1,082
Inca dove	11					
Island turtle-dove	4					
White-winged dove	40	3		2	102	2,054
Common ground-dove	6					
Parrots	**19**			**2**		
Parrots	3			1		
Budgerigar	11					
Monk parakeet	4			1		
Nanday parakeet	1					

Table 17. Continued (Page 9 of 20)

Wildlife group or species	23-year totals (1990–2012)					
	Number of reported strikes				Reported economic losses[1]	
	Total	With damage	With neg. EOF	With multiple animals[2]	Aircraft down time (hrs)	Reported costs ($)
Cuckoos/roadrunners	**28**	**5**	**1**	**4**	**37**	**117,563**
Cuckoos	4	2		1	12	76,495
Yellow-billed cuckoo	21	3	1	3	25	41,068
Common cuckoo	1					
Black-billed cuckoo	1					
Greater roadrunner	1					
Owls	**1,945**	**113**	**71**	**21**	**1,970**	**7,771,897**
Owls	292	30	19	4	963	489,302
Barn owl	884	35	24	11	301	2,780,755
Snowy owl	84	8	6		147	444,009
Little owl	1					
Short-eared owl	359	9	10	3	83	1,410,570
Long-eared owl	13	3	1		24	51,336
Northern saw-whet owl	6					
Burrowing owl	118	1		2	8	805
Barred owl	18	1	1			162
Northern pygmy-owl	1					
Great gray owl	1					
Eastern screech-owl	3	2			24	13,147
Western screech-owl	2					
Great horned owl	162	24	10	1	420	2,581,811
Northern hawk owl	1					
Nightjars	**352**	**3**	**3**	**22**	**68**	
Nightjars	4					
Whip-poor-will	6			2		
Common poorwill	8					
Lesser nighthawk	7					
Chuck-will's-widow	6		1		1	
Common nighthawk	319	3	2	20	67	
Common pauraque	2					
Swifts	**324**	**8**	**6**	**27**	**42**	**1,886**
Swifts	7	1		1		
Black swift	3					
Chimney swift	266	5	5	25	16	1,886
Common swift	3	1				
Vaux's swift	25				24	
White-throated swift	20	1	1	1	2	

Table 17. Continued (Page 10 of 20)

Wildlife group or species	23-year totals (1990–2012)					
	Number of reported strikes				Reported economic losses[1]	
	Total	With damage	With neg. EOF	With multiple animals[2]	Aircraft down time (hrs)	Reported costs ($)
Hummingbirds	**16**					
Hummingbirds	1					
Ruby-thrtd hummingbird	7					
Anna's hummingbird	5					
Bk-chinned hummingbird	1					
Allen's hummingbird	1					
Calliope hummingbird	1					
Belted kingfisher	**9**					
Woodpeckers	**110**	**7**	**7**	**3**	**180**	**23,531**
Woodpeckers	12		1			
Northern flicker	64	4	1	1	10	2,238
Yellow-bellied sapsucker	27	2	2	2	169	2,772
Hairy woodpecker	3					
Red-naped sapsucker	2	1	2			18,521
Downy woodpecker	2		1		1	
Unidentified passeriformes	**306**	**11**	**10**	**28**	**83**	**113,894**
Flycatchers	**346**	**1**	**5**	**25**	**2**	**13,196**
Tyrant flycatchers	24			5	1	
Eastern wood-pewee	3					
Great crested flycatcher	5					
Eastern kingbird	19	1	1			13,096
Scissor-tailed flycatcher	125		3	7		100
Acadian flycatcher	3					
Say's phoebe	5					
Western kingbird	139		1	11	1	
Ash-throated flycatcher	1					
Western wood-pewee	2					
Sulphur-bellied flycatcher	1					
Eastern phoebe	5					
Yellow-bellied flycatcher	1			1		
Least flycatcher	2					
Hammond's flycatcher	1					
Pacific-slope flycatcher	4					
Gray flycatcher	2			1		
Olive-sided flycatcher	1					
White-crested elaenia	1					
Willow flycatcher	1					
Alder flycatcher	1					

Table 17. Continued (Page 11 of 20)

Wildlife group or species	23-year totals (1990–2012)					
	Number of reported strikes				Reported economic losses[1]	
	Total	With damage	With neg. EOF	With multiple animals[2]	Aircraft down time (hrs)	Reported costs ($)
Larks	**2,247**	**16**	**30**	**392**	**194**	**888,746**
Sky lark	57			1		
Horned lark	2,190	16	30	391	194	888,746
Swallows	**4,718**	**31**	**80**	**1,054**	**367**	**165,173**
Swallows	818	7	31	252	50	81
Purple martin	132	7	3	35	53	87,665
Bank swallow	227	2	4	91	7	2,053
Barn swallow	2,303	11	30	426	217	56,214
Cliff swallow	774	3	8	123	28	19,080
Tree swallow	410		4	123	10	80
Violet-green swallow	16			1		
N. rough-winged swallow	30	1		1	2	
Cave swallow	8			2		
Black drongo	**7**					
Starlings/mynas	**3,142**	**111**	**160**	**1,152**	**2,835**	**6,861,993**
European starling	3,064	110	156	1,129	2,830	6,861,993
Common myna	78	1	4	23	5	
Crows/ravens	**609**	**61**	**53**	**81**	**9,612**	**2,107,860**
Crows, ravens	1	1		1		
Crows	189	20	15	34	18	122,799
American crow	374	30	31	42	6,453	1,784,677
Carrion crow	2					
Hooded crow	1	1	1			
Northwestern crow	6			1		
Rook	1					
Common raven	35	9	6	3	3,141	200,384
Jays/magpies	**35**	**2**	**2**	**5**	**2**	**916**
Blue jay	17			1	1	
Gray jay	1					
Yellow-billed magpie	8			2		
Black-billed magpie	9	2	2	2	1	916
Chickadees/nuthatches	**31**	**1**		**9**		
Chickadees	1					
Black-capped chickadee	22	1		6		
Mountain chickadee	2			1		
Gray-headed chickadee	1			1		
Carolina chickadee	2			1		
Bushtit	2					

Table 17. Continued (Page 12 of 20)

Wildlife group or species	23-year totals (1990–2012)					
	Number of reported strikes				Reported economic losses[1]	
	Total	With damage	With neg. EOF	With multiple animals[2]	Aircraft down time (hrs)	Reported costs ($)
White-breasted nuthatch	1					
Red-vented bulbul	**3**			**1**		
Wrens	**83**	**1**	**2**	**10**	**1**	
Wrens	46	1	1	9		
Marsh wren	9		1			
House wren	15			1		
Carolina wren	4					
Rock wren	1					
Cactus wren	3					
Winter wren	3				1	
Bewick's wren	1					
Sedge wren	1					
Mimics	**135**	**1**	**2**	**5**	**6**	**761**
Brown thrasher	10					220
Curve-billed thrasher	1					
Northern mockingbird	72	1	2			
Tropical mockingbird	1					
Gray catbird	51			5	6	541
Thrushes	**821**	**60**	**36**	**64**	**2,082**	**3,266,658**
Thrushes	24	3	1	1	7	32,327
Western bluebird	4				3	
Swainson's thrush	80	7	2	7	27	2,471,982
Redwing	1					
American robin	582	41	24	41	1,972	739,480
Hermit thrush	49	2	3	3	40	4,451
Eastern bluebird	5			1		
Gray-cheeked thrush	12		1	2		
Varied thrush	32	7	2	5	31	18,072
Wood thrush	11		1	2		346
Mountain bluebird	11			2		
Veery	10		2		2	
Wrentits/gnatcatchers	**9**		**1**		**2**	
Wrentit	1					
Blue-gray gnatcatcher	8		1		2	
Kinglets	**43**		**2**	**3**		
Golden-crowned kinglet	13					
Ruby-crowned kinglet	30		2	3		

Table 17. Continued (Page 13 of 20)

Wildlife group or species	23-year totals (1990–2012)					
	Number of reported strikes				Reported economic losses[1]	
	Total	With dam-age	With neg. EOF	With multiple animals[2]	Aircraft down time (hrs)	Reported costs ($)
Pipits	**54**			**13**		
American pipit	51			13		
Sprague's pipit	3					
Waxwings	**82**	**3**	**4**	**17**	**49**	**174,994**
Bohemian waxwing	1			1		
Cedar waxwing	81	3	4	16	49	174,994
Loggerhead shrike	**13**		**1**			
Vireos	**52**	**2**	**1**	**3**	**8**	**8,484**
Vireos	4					
White-eyed vireo	2				2	
Blue-headed vireo	1					
Yellow-throated vireo	1					
Warbling vireo	13	1		1	3	8,484
Red-eyed vireo	28	1	1	2	3	
Cassin's vireo	2					
Philadelphia vireo	1					
Japanese white-eye	**2**					
Warblers	**397**	**4**	**10**	**27**	**83**	**18,146**
Wood warblers	49	1		5		1,889
Canada warbler	12		2		2	103
Yellow-breasted chat	5					
Pine warbler	9			1		
Black-and-white warbler	11					
Northern parula	5			1	24	2,108
Ovenbird	31	1	2		3	1,140
Wilson's warbler	21			1	4	5,077
Common yellowthroat	24		1		2	
Yellow-rumped warbler	62			8	5	50
Blackpoll warbler	23			3	2	492
Mourning warbler	3					
American redstart	12	1		2	11	
Orange-crowned warbler	11					
Yellow warbler	18	1		1	17	
Cape May warbler	1					
Northern waterthrush	11					
Nashville warbler	12		1	1		
Townsend's warbler	6		1	1		100
Palm warbler	14		2	1	3	7,187

Table 17. Continued (Page 14 of 20)

Wildlife group or species	23-year totals (1990–2012)					
	Number of reported strikes				Reported economic losses[1]	
	Total	With damage	With neg. EOF	With multiple animals[2]	Aircraft down time (hrs)	Reported costs ($)
Magnolia warbler	18		1		6	
Bk-throated blue warbler	4					
Prothonotary warbler	2					
MacGillivray's warbler	3					
Yellow-throated warbler	9			1		
Bk-throated gray warbler	2				2	
Bk-thrtd green warbler	3					
Hermit warbler	1					
Tennessee warbler	6				2	
Chestnut-sided warbler	3					
Blackburnian warbler	3					
Bay-breasted warbler	2			1		
Connecticut warbler	1					
Meadowlarks	**2,007**	**20**	**39**	**207**	**376**	**498,008**
Meadowlarks	375	3	10	38	14	513
Eastern meadowlark	948	6	16	83	142	142,640
Western meadowlark	684	11	13	86	220	354,855
Blackbirds/grackles	**1,922**	**105**	**120**	**487**	**1,529**	**1,700,275**
Blackbirds/grackles	1,263	79	89	360	607	1,411,553
Red-winged blackbird	186	5	9	23	8	3,137
Yellow-headed blackbird	10	1	1	2		
Brewer's blackbird	40	1	1	7	1	
Brown-headed cowbird	138	2	3	41	11	6,038
Bobolink	17		1	2	2	
Rusty blackbird	2					
Tricolored blackbird	1					
Grackles	107	9	3	23	728	207,494
Common grackle	111	5	9	24	124	72,053
Boat-tailed grackle	15	2	3	1	48	
Great-tailed grackle	32	1	1	4		
Orioles	**25**	**1**	**2**	**2**	**2**	**211**
Orioles	5					
Baltimore oriole	14	1	2	2	2	211
Orchard oriole	3					
Bullock's oriole	3					
Tanagers	**13**	**1**	**1**		**3**	
Scarlet tanager	5	1				
Western tanager	8		1		3	

Table 17. Continued (Page 15 of 20)

Wildlife group or species	23-year totals (1990–2012)					
	Number of reported strikes				Reported economic losses[1]	
	Total	With dam-age	With neg. EOF	With multiple animals[2]	Aircraft down time (hrs)	Reported costs ($)
Finches	**681**	**8**	**33**	**213**	**200**	**25,015**
Finches	70	1	4	19	5	
Lapland longspur	35		3	13	25	
Chnt-collared longspur	2					
Dark-eyed junco	63	2	2	6	75	11,072
Rose-breasted grosbeak	5				1	513
Island canary	1					
Pine siskin	12	1		5	1	
Purple finch	3					
Red crossbill	2			1		
Evening grosbeak	1					
American goldfinch	44		2	2	3	
House finch	75		1	7	2	
Smith's longspur	2					
Dickcissel	8			1		
White-winged crossbill	1					
Red avadavat	5			3		
McCown's longspur	1					
Lesser goldfinch	3					
Black-headed grosbeak	3					
Cassin's finch	1					
Pine grosbeak	1					
Red-crested cardinal	5			1	1	
Northern cardinal	11					
Snow bunting	213	3	19	135	82	13,430
Indigo bunting	9		1	2	3	
Lazuli bunting	1					
Lark bunting	101	1		16	2	
McKay's bunting	1		1	1		
Painted bunting	1					
Black-faced bunting	1			1		
Sparrows	**3,406**	**55**	**110**	**738**	**715**	**117,712**
Sparrows	2,772	47	103	682	649	68,456
Harris's sparrow	2			1		
Swamp sparrow	23			1		
Savannah sparrow	235	3	1	17	16	7,574
Fox sparrow	27	1			1	5,625
White-throated sparrow	77	1	1	9	14	2,242

Table 17. Continued (Page 16 of 20)

Wildlife group or species	23-year totals (1990–2012)					
	Number of reported strikes				Reported economic losses[1]	
	Total	With damage	With neg. EOF	With multiple animals[2]	Aircraft down time (hrs)	Reported costs ($)
Golden-crowned sparrow	3			1		
Field sparrow	23			2		
Lark sparrow	17			2		
White-crowned sparrow	23	1	2	1	25	
Grasshopper sparrow	35	1	1	2	4	33,002
Java sparrow	3			1		
Vesper sparrow	27			1		
Chipping sparrow	28	1		3		103
Lincoln's sparrow	15		1	1		
Song sparrow	70			11	4	494
Sage sparrow	6				1	
American tree sparrow	10		1	2		
N's sharp-tailed sparrow	3				1	216
Black-throated sparrow	1					
Brewer's sparrow	4			1		
Le Conte's sparrow	1					
Cassin's sparrow	1					
Towhees	**9**	**1**			**9**	**14,614**
Eastern towhee	7	1			9	14,614
Green-tailed towhee	1					
California towhee	1					
Waxbills/mannikins	**243**		**1**	**69**	**10**	**4,956**
Waxbills/mannikins	3					
Common waxbill	4					
Mannikins	126			14		
Nutmeg mannikin	60			30	8	1,825
Black-headed munia	46		1	22	2	3,131
White-throated munia	4			3		
House sparrow	**146**	**3**	**2**	**14**	**28**	**2,168**
Total known birds	**62,421**	**5,942**	**4,690**	**11,625**	**381,214**	**451,290,440**
Total unknown birds	**64,791**	**5,939**	**3,699**	**6,781**	**136,177**	**126,193,645**
Unknown bird - ? size	2,809	243	210	149	5,408	1,475,902
Unknown bird - large	2,424	966	461	267	42,021	45,022,290
Unknown bird - medium	33,139	3,912	2,038	2,619	76,897	62,564,978
Unknown bird - small	26,419	818	990	3,746	11,851	17,130,475
Total birds[3]	**127,212**	**11,881**	**8,389**	**18,406**	**517,391**	**577,484,085**

Table 17. Continued (Page 17 of 20)

Wildlife group or species	23-year totals (1990–2012)					
	Number of reported strikes				Reported economic losses[1]	
	Total	With dam-age	With neg. EOF	With multiple animals[2]	Aircraft down time (hrs)	Reported costs ($)
Flying mammals (bats)						
Megabats (fruit bats)	**13**	**2**	**2**	**4**	**99**	**4,443,944**
Microbats (echo-locating)	**766**	**7**	**6**	**52**	**41**	**1,413**
Microbats (unkn species)	448	5	3	39	31	
Vesper bats	23				1	
Red bat	48	1		3	1	
Hoary bat	15				1	
E. small-footed myotis	1					
Little brown bat	42			1		
Big brown bat	30		1	2		
Silver-haired bat	17			1	2	308
Seminole bat	2					
Eastern pipistrelle	4					
Northern yellow bat	3					
Evening bat	2					
Free-tailed bats	28			2		300
Brazilian free-tailed bat	98	1	2	4	5	805
Pocketed free-tailed bat	2					
Big free-tailed bat	1					
Western mastiff bat	1					
Florida bonneted bat	1					
Total known bats	**779**	**9**	**8**	**56**	**140**	**4,445,357**
Total unkn-Mega or Micro	**3**	**1**				**9,568**
Total bats[4]	**782**	**10**	**8**	**56**	**140**	**4,454,925**
Terrestrial mammals						
Marsupials (Vir. opossum)	**140**	**1**		**1**		
Xenarthyras (armadillo)	**27**	**1**	**5**		**11**	**1,269**
Lagomorphs	**434**	**7**	**8**	**7**	**20**	**127,176**
Lagomorphs	1	1				
Hares	6					
Black-tailed jackrabbit	210	3	2	1	12	33,370
White-tailed jackrabbit	37			2	1	
Antelope jackrabbit	1					
Rabbits	94		2	4	1	
Eastern cottontail	65	3	4		6	93,806
Desert cottontail	20					

Table 17. Continued (Page 18 of 20)

Wildlife group or species	23-year totals (1990–2012)					
	Number of reported strikes				Reported economic losses[1]	
	Total	With damage	With neg. EOF	With multiple animals[2]	Aircraft down time (hrs)	Reported costs ($)
Rodents	**209**	**2**	**6**	**5**	**3**	
North American beaver	2					
Black-tailed prairie dog	38			2		
White-tailed prairie dog	5					
Gunnison's prairie dog	15		1	3		
Woodchuck	116	2	5		3	
Yellow-bellied marmot	1					
Fox squirrel	1					
Muskrat	20					
N. American porcupine	11					
Carnivores	**1,032**	**61**	**130**	**14**	**14,859**	**4,099,192**
Canids	3		1			
Coyote	406	37	86	5	12,249	3,599,069
Domestic dog	39	11	20	1	96	382,711
Foxes	64	4	7	1	10	1,057
Red fox	121	3	10		340	57,782
Common gray fox	7	1	1		2	269
Kit fox	3					
Raccoon	84	4	3	2	2,160	58,304
White-nosed coati	1					
Ringtail	1					
Skunks	52		1	2	2	
Striped skunk	209			3		
River otter	2	1				
Badger	4					
Mink	4					
Domestic cat	28					
Small Indian mongoose	3					
American black bear	1		1			
Artiodactyls	**1,079**	**915**	**503**	**91**	**282,562**	**53,203,195**
Deer	22	20	11		696	268,757
White-tailed deer	950	798	436	80	233,265	43,555,623
Mule deer	65	59	31	3	19,908	1,179,617
Wapiti (elk)	11	11	6	1	11,660	7,428,745
Moose	5	4	4			
Caribou	2	2	1			
Cattle	11	11	8	4	9,215	495,150
Pronghorn	9	8	5	2	5,130	239,150

Table 17. Continued (Page 19 of 20)

Wildlife group or species	23-year totals (1990–2012)					
	Number of reported strikes				Reported economic losses[1]	
	Total	With damage	With neg. EOF	With multiple animals[2]	Aircraft down time (hrs)	Reported costs ($)
Swine (pigs)	2	1			2,688	36,153
Collared peccary	2	1	1	1		
Perissodactyls	**4**	**4**	**3**		**1,008**	**36,361**
Horse	3	3	3		1,008	36,361
Burro	1	1				
Total known t. mammals	**2,925**	**991**	**655**	**118**	**298,463**	**57,467,193**
Total unknown t. mammals	**21**	**6**	**8**	**1**		
Total terrestrial mammals[5]	**2,946**	**997**	**663**	**119**	**298,463**	**57,467,193**
Reptiles						
Turtles	**130**	**1**	**2**	**2**		
Turtles (unkn species)	70	1	2	1		
Florida soft shell turtle	4					
Eastern box turtle	7					
Common snapping turtle	6					
Diamondback terrapin	32			1		
Painted turtle	5					
Florida red-bellied cooter	1					
Gopher tortoise	3					
Alligator snapping turtle	1					
Florida cooter	1					
American alligator	**18**	**1**	**2**		**3**	
Green iguana	**8**		**4**			
Total reptiles[6]	**156**	**2**	**8**	**2**	**3**	
Total known (all species)	**66,281**	**6,944**	**5,361**	**11,801**	**679,820**	**513,202,990**
Total (unknown species)	**64,815**	**5,946**	**3,707**	**6,782**	**136,177**	**126,203,213**
Grand total	**131,096**	**12,890**	**9,068**	**18,583**	**815,997**	**639,406,203[7]**

[1] These reported economic losses by species and species groups should be considered as relative indices of losses and not as actual estimated losses. For commercial aviation, an estimated 20 percent of strikes were reported in the 1990s and about 39 percent from 2004-2008. General aviation reporting rates are much lower than for commercial aviation. In addition, only about 48 percent of reported strikes identified the wildlife species or species group responsible, 1990–2012. Furthermore, of the 12,291 reports indicating damage to the aircraft, only 26 percent (3,194) also provided an estimate of repair costs, and only 49 percent (6,015) estimated the downtime (see Table 22). Finally, even when cost estimates were provided, many reports were filed before aircraft damage had been fully assessed. See Tables 22 and 23 for a more detailed projection of actual economic losses.

Table 17. Continued (Page 20 of 20)

[2] More than 1 animal was struck by the aircraft.

[3] Of the 127,212 reported bird strikes, 45,295 (36 percent) identified the bird to exact species (482 species total of which 222 caused damage) and an additional 17,126 strikes (13 percent) identified the bird at least to species group. Species identification has improved from less than 20 percent in the early 1990s to 56 percent in 2012 (Figure 7).

[4] Of the 782 reported bat strikes, 267 (34 percent) identified the bat to exact species (15 species total of which 2 caused damage) and 512 (65 percent) identified the bat to species group (13 megabats [old world fruit bats], 499 microbats [echo-locating bats]). There were 3 bat strikes classified as unknown bat (either megabat or microbat).

[5] Of the 2,946 reported terrestrial mammal strikes, 2,683 (91 percent) identified the mammal to exact species (42 species total of which 22 caused damage) and 242 (8 percent) identified the mammal at least to species group.

[6] All of the 156 reported reptile strikes were identified to species group and 86 (55 percent) were identified to exact species (11 species total of which 2 caused damage).

[7] Reported costs of $639,406,203 include $571,427,187 in direct repair costs and $67,979,016 in other costs (see Tables 22 and 23).

Table 18. Number of reported strikes, strikes with damage, and strikes involving multiple animals for the four most commonly struck bird groups and three most commonly struck terrestrial mammal groups, civil aircraft, USA, 1990–2012.

Species group[1]	Reported strikes		Strikes with damage		Strikes with >1 animal	
	23-year total	% of total known	23-year total	% of total known	23-year total	% of total known
Birds						
Gulls	9,252	15	1,321	22	2,021	17
Pigeons/ doves	9,141	15	440	7	1,990	17
Raptors[2]	8,185	13	1,189	20	318	3
Waterfowl	4,137	7	1,767	30	1,477	13
All other known	31,706	51	1,225	21	5,819	50
Total known birds	**62,421**	**100**	**5,942**	**100**	**11,625**	**100**
Unknown birds	**64,791**		**5,939**		**6,781**	
Total birds	**127,212**		**11,881**		**18,406**	
Terrestrial mammals						
Artiodactyls	1,079	37	915	92	91	77
Carnivores	1,032	35	61	6	14	12
Lagomorphs	434	15	7	1	7	6
All other known	380	13	8	1	6	5
Total known t. mammals	**2,925**	**100**	**991**	**100**	**118**	**100**
Unknown t. mammals	**21**		**6**		**1**	
Total t. mammals	**2,946**		**997**		**119**	

[1] See Table 17 for listing of species within each species group.

[2] Hawks, eagles, vultures, falcons, and caracaras.

Table 19. Ranking of hazard level of 86 bird and 10 terrestrial mammal species with 50 or more reported strikes with civil aircraft in USA, 1990–2012 (Table 17), based on a composite of the percent of strikes causing damage, major damage, and a negative effect-on-flight (EOF) (page 1 of 3)[1,2].

| Hazard rank | Wildlife species | Total reported strikes | Percent of strikes with: | | | Mean hazard level[3] |
			Damage	Major damage	Neg. EOF	
	Birds					
1	Snow goose	109	77	41	39	53
2	Black vulture	93	63	30	41	45
3	Turkey vulture	487	51	19	35	35
4	Northern pintail	116	51	17	30	33
5	Canada goose	1,400	50	17	28	31
6	Brown pelican	59	42	14	36	31
7	Sandhill crane	111	41	13	27	27
8	Bald eagle	155	41	12	28	27
9	American wigeon	51	45	14	16	25
10	Double-crested cormorant	100	34	15	24	24
11	Northern shoveler	53	43	15	13	24
12	Wild turkey	57	33	5	26	22
13	Ring-necked pheasant	75	23	12	17	17
14	Mallard	688	23	9	13	15
15	Osprey	240	22	7	15	15
16	Great blue heron	305	21	6	16	15
17	American coot	147	24	7	11	14
18	Glaucous-winged gull	89	21	3	12	12
19	Great egret	62	18	3	13	11
20	Red-tailed hawk	1,659	15	5	11	10
21	California gull	115	11	7	10	10
22	Cattle egret	269	10	3	15	9
23	Western gull	100	11	7	7	8
24	Swainson's hawk	78	13	3	9	8
25	Great horned owl	162	15	3	6	8
26	Herring gull	996	10	5	9	8
27	Great black-backed gull	95	11	6	6	8
27	Rock pigeon	2,333	10	4	10	8
29	Snowy owl	84	10	5	7	7
30	Mew gull	57	11	2	7	6
31	Ring-billed gull	1,193	8	3	8	6
31	Franklin's gull	85	5	5	9	6
31	American crow	374	8	3	8	6
34	Rough-legged hawk	64	8	3	5	5

Table 19. Continued (Page 2 of 3)

Hazard rank	Wildlife species	Total reported strikes	Percent of strikes with:			Mean hazard level[3]
			Damage	Major damage	Neg. EOF	
	Birds (continued)					
35	Peregrine falcon	224	8	2	5	5
36	Blk-crowned night-heron	57	7	4	4	5
37	Swainson's thrush	80	9	3	3	5
38	Laughing gull	337	5	2	7	5
38	Common grackle	111	5	<1	8	5
40	Western sandpiper	70	6	0	7	4
41	Black-bellied plover	97	6	1	5	4
42	American robin	582	7	<1	4	4
43	Wilson's snipe	54	6	0	6	4
44	Cooper's hawk	56	5	0	5	4
44	Snow bunting	213	1	<1	9	4
46	European starling	3,064	4	1	5	3
47	American golden-plover	108	4	2	4	3
48	Merlin	58	2	2	5	3
48	Upland sandpiper	164	4	1	4	3
48	Barn owl	884	4	2	3	3
48	Cedar waxwing	81	4	0	5	3
52	Purple martin	132	5	<1	2	3
53	Dark-eyed junco	63	3	2	3	3
54	American woodcock	51	4	0	4	3
54	Least sandpiper	78	1	0	6	3
54	Mourning dove	5,362	3	<1	4	3
54	Northern flicker	64	6	0	2	3
58	Red-winged blackbird	186	3	0	5	3
59	Spotted dove	174	2	1	3	2
60	Short-eared owl	359	3	1	3	2
60	Common myna	78	1	0	5	2
62	Northern harrier	102	2	1	2	2
63	Northern mockingbird	72	1	0	3	1
63	Western meadowlark	684	2	<1	2	1
63	Brown-headed cowbird	138	1	<1	2	1
66	Chimney swift	266	2	0	2	1
66	White-throated sparrow	77	1	1	1	1
68	Killdeer	2,920	1	<1	2	1
68	House sparrow	146	2	0	1	1
70	Zebra dove	263	1	<1	2	1
71	American kestrel	3,236	<1	<1	2	<1
71	Bank swallow	227	<1	0	2	<1
71	Eastern meadowlark	948	<1	<1	2	<1

Table 19. Continued (page 3 of 3).

Hazard rank	Wildlife species	Total reported strikes	Percent of strikes with:			Mean hazard level[3]
			Damage	Major damage	Neg. EOF	
	Birds (continued)					
74	Scissor-tailed flycatcher	125	0	0	2	<1
75	Pacific golden-plover	753	<1	0	1	<1
75	Horned lark	2,190	<1	<1	1	<1
75	Lark bunting	101	1	1	0	<1
78	Barn swallow	2,303	<1	0	1	<1
78	Savannah sparrow	235	1	0	<1	<1
80	Common nighthawk	319	<1	0	<1	<1
80	Cliff swallow	774	<1	<1	1	<1
82	House finch	75	0	0	1	<1
83	Burrowing owl	118	<1	0	0	<1
83	Tree swallow	410	0	0	1	<1
85	Western kingbird	139	0	0	<1	<1
86	Semipalmated plover	57	0	0	0	0
86	Sky lark	57	0	0	0	0
86	Gray catbird	51	0	0	0	0
86	American pipit	51	0	0	0	0
86	Yellow-rumped warbler	62	0	0	0	0
86	Song sparrow	70	0	0	0	0
86	Nutmeg mannikin	60	0	0	0	0
	Terrestrial mammals					
1	Mule deer	65	91	35	48	58
2	White-tailed deer	950	84	36	46	55
3	Coyote	406	9	2	21	11
4	Eastern cottontail	65	5	2	6	4
5	Red fox	121	3	0	8	4
5	Raccoon	84	5	2	4	4
7	Woodchuck	116	2	0	4	2
8	Black-tailed jackrabbit	210	1	<1	1	1
9	Virginia opossum	140	<1	0	0	<1
10	Striped skunk	209	0	0	0	0

[1] See Dolbeer and Wright (2009) and DeVault et al. (2011) for more detailed discussions of the use of wildlife strike data to rank species as to their hazard level to air operations and for use in airport Wildlife Hazard Management Plans and Safety Management Systems.

[2] Wildlife species with fewer than 50 reported strikes are not listed in this table. This does not imply that unlisted species are not hazardous to aircraft. The hazard level of unlisted species can be approximated by using the hazard level of similar species in this table.

[3] Based on the mean value for percent of strikes with damage, major damage (substantial damage or destroyed, Table 13), and negative effect-on-flight (Table 14).

Table 20. The mean hazard level and hazard level rank (out of 86) of the 25 species of birds most frequently struck by civil aircraft in USA, 1990-2012.

Rank (number. of strikes)	Bird species	Number of strikes	Mean hazard level[1]	Rank (hazard level)[1]
1	Mourning dove	5,362	3	54
2	American kestrel	3,236	<1	71
3	European starling	3,064	3	46
4	Killdeer	2,920	1	68
5	Rock pigeon	2,333	8	27
6	Barn swallow	2,303	<1	78
7	Horned lark	2,190	<1	75
8	Red-tailed hawk	1,659	10	20
9	Canada goose	1,400	31	5
10	Ring-billed gull	1,193	6	31
11	Herring gull	996	8	26
12	Eastern meadowlark	948	<1	71
13	Barn owl	884	3	48
14	Cliff swallow	774	<1	80
15	Pacific golden-plover	753	<1	75
16	Mallard	688	15	14
17	Western meadowlark	684	1	63
18	American robin	582	4	42
19	Turkey vulture	487	35	3
20	Tree swallow	410	<1	83
21	American crow	374	6	31
22	Short-eared owl	359	2	60
23	Laughing gull	337	5	38
24	Common nighthawk	319	<1	80
25	Great blue heron	305	15	16

[1] Mean hazard level is based on composite of percentage of strikes causing damage, major damage, and a negative effect on flight. Hazard ranking (1 = most hazardous) is for the 86 bird species with at least 50 reported strikes, 1990-2012 (see Table 19).

Table 21. Number of strikes to civil aircraft causing human fatality or injury and number of injuries and fatalities by wildlife species, USA, 1990–2012.

Species of wildlife	No. of strikes	No. of humans		Species of wildlife	No. of strikes	No. of humans
Strikes causing fatalities				**Strikes causing injuries (continued)**		
Unknown bird	5	7		Snow goose	3	3
White-tailed deer	1	1		Grebes	1	2
Brown pelican	1	1		Osprey	2	2
Amer. white pelican	1	5		Red-throated loon	1	2
Canada goose	1	2		Sharp-tailed grouse	1	2
Red-tailed hawk	1	8		American robin	1	1
Total (fatalities)	**10**	**24**		Cackling goose	1	1
				Doves	1	1
Strikes causing injuries				Egrets	1	1
Unknown bird	39	49		Franklin's gull	1	1
Canada goose	15	18		Frigatebirds	1	1
Ducks	15	18		Great frigatebird	1	1
Turkey vulture	14	17		Great-tailed grackle	1	1
Black vulture	7	11		Horned grebe	1	1
New World Vultures	10	10		Long-tailed duck	1	1
Gulls	8	9		Mourning dove	1	1
Red-tailed hawk	6	8		Owls	1	1
Ring-billed gull	2	8		Red-tailed tropicbird	1	1
Bald eagle	4	7		Sandhill crane	1	1
Geese	7	7		Snowy egret	1	1
Mallard	5	6		Sparrows	1	1
American kestrel	1	5		Tropicbirds	1	1
Hawks	3	5		Western grebe	1	1
Anhinga	3	4		White ibis	1	1
Eurasian kestrel	1	4				
Golden eagle	2	4		White-tailed deer	19	27
Lesser scaup	4	4		Cattle	2	3
Spotted dove	1	4		Domestic dog	1	2
American coot	3	3		Mule deer	1	2
D.-crsted cormorant	3	3		Eastern cottontail	1	1
Herring gull	3	3		Horse	1	1
Rock pigeon	3	3		**Total (injuries)**	**211**	**276**

Table 22. Number of civil aircraft lost (destroyed or damaged beyond repair) after striking wildlife by wildlife species and aircraft mass category, USA, 1990–2012[1].

Wildlife species or species group	Aircraft[2] mass category (Maximum takeoff mass)				Total aircraft lost
	≤2,250 kg	2,251-5,700 kg	5,701-27,000 kg	>27,000 kg	
White-tailed deer	14	5	2		21
Unknown bird	10	2	1		13
Canada goose	1	3		1	5
Cattle	2	1			3
Turkey vulture	2				2
Hawks	2				2
Eastern cottontail	1				1
Coyote			1		1
Domestic dog	1				1
Wapiti (elk)			1		1
Brown pelican	1				1
Amer. white pelican		1			1
D.-crested cormorant	1				1
Ducks	1				1
New World Vultures	1				1
Bald eagle	1				1
Red-tailed hawk		1			1
Eurasian kestrel				1	1
Ring-billed gull		1			1
Mourning dove			1		1
Total	**38**	**14**	**6**	**2**	**60**

[1] Forty (67 percent) of the 60 wildlife strikes resulting in a destroyed aircraft occurred at General Aviation airports, 12 occurred "en-route", 6 occurred at USA airports certificated for passenger service under 14 CFR Part 139, and 2 occurred at a foreign airport certificated for passenger service.

[2] Engine types on the 60 destroyed aircraft were piston (44), turbofan (7), turboprop (5), turbojet (2), and turboshaft (2). Aircraft operator was business (32), private (22), commercial transport (5), and Government (1).

Table 23. Number of reported wildlife strikes indicating damage, a negative effect-on-flight (EOF), aircraft downtime, repair costs, and other costs; and the mean losses per report in hours of downtime and inflation-adjusted U.S. dollars, for civil aircraft, USA, 1990–2012.

	Number of reports indicating:					Mean losses per report		
Year	Dam-age	Neg. EOF	Aircraft down time	Repair costs	Other costs	Down-time (hours)	Repair costs ($)	Other costs ($)
1990	372	146	61	33	16	55.6	211,170	60,619
1991	401	187	61	48	25	79.8	73,991	39,181
1992	368	221	81	51	28	111.9	104,344	5,250
1993	399	240	67	57	19	277.9	89,077	9,385
1994	463	274	103	73	28	388.4	76,504	94,611
1995	499	310	95	62	31	104.3	505,935	234,212
1996	504	372	144	84	39	137.3	81,399	25,357
1997	582	387	184	126	47	228.2	76,123	39,847
1998	588	403	205	137	54	119.5	197,307	28,294
1999	706	447	284	176	79	147.8	109,960	20,596
2000	764	477	352	206	93	195.0	152,947	113,353
2001	649	436	293	156	64	156.2	283,727	39,267
2002	674	504	387	167	64	134.2	147,576	61,968
2003	634	442	359	172	82	110.8	157,232	41,278
2004	628	433	325	213	92	172.2	103,485	22,213
2005	609	458	329	226	126	87.5	264,135	75,221
2006	598	432	333	172	102	116.8	212,270	13,201
2007	571	458	366	178	135	164.3	170,955	32,920
2008	530	412	373	158	143	115.6	116,934	13,880
2009	607	522	563	195	193	80.8	364,037	14,259
2010	598	468	529	175	165	65.0	124,469	13,218
2011	541	500	526	179	206	70.8	227,077	14,749
2012	605	539	683	218	261	75.8	104,201	8,061
Total	**12,890**	**9,068**	**6,703**	**3,262**	**2,092**			
Mean	**560**	**394**	**291**	**142**	**91**	**121.7**	**175,177**	**32,495**

Table 24. Projected annual losses in aircraft downtime (hours) and in repair and other costs (inflation-adjusted U.S. dollars) caused by wildlife strikes with civil aircraft, USA, 1990–2012. Losses are projected from mean reported losses per incident (see Table 23).

Year	No. of adverse incidents[3]	Minimum projected losses[1]				Maximum projected losses[2]	
		Down-time (hours)	Repair costs (x $1 million)	Other costs (x $1 million)	Total costs (x $1 million)	Down-time (hours)	Total costs (x $1 million)
1990	427	23,758	90	26	116	118,790	580
1991	487	38,840	36	19	55	194,201	276
1992	497	55,627	52	3	54	278,136	272
1993	509	141,456	45	5	50	707,282	251
1994	585	227,236	45	55	100	1,136,178	501
1995	659	68,723	333	154	488	343,616	2,439
1996	690	94,717	56	18	74	473,584	368
1997	791	180,490	60	32	92	902,449	459
1998	811	96,916	160	23	183	484,582	915
1999	982	145,111	108	20	128	725,556	641
2000	1,114	217,274	170	126	297	1,086,372	1,483
2001	981	153,274	278	39	317	766,369	1,584
2002	1,111	149,127	164	69	233	745,633	1,164
2003	1,005	111,334	158	41	200	556,669	998
2004	956	164,603	99	21	120	823,013	601
2005	982	85,903	259	74	333	429,513	1,666
2006	944	110,261	200	12	213	551,305	1,064
2007	982	161,381	168	32	200	806,903	1,001
2008	912	105,391	107	13	119	526,955	597
2009	1,192	96,317	434	17	451	481,585	2,255
2010	1,130	73,486	141	15	156	367,432	778
2011	1,145	81,036	260	17	277	405,180	1,384
2012	1,324	100,345	138	11	149	501,724	743
Total	**20,216**	**2,682,606**	**3,562**	**841**	**4,404**	**13,413,028**	**22,019**
Mean	**879**	**116,635**	**155**	**36**	**191**	**583,175**	**957**

[1] Minimum values are based on the assumption that all 20,216 reported strikes (mean of 879/year) indicating an adverse effect (see footnote 3) incurred similar amounts of damage and/or downtime and

Table 24. Continued (Page 2 of 2).

that these reports are all of the adverse-effect strikes that occurred, 1990–2012.

[2] Analyses of strike data from 1991-2004 indicated that 11 to 21 percent of strikes were reported for air carrier aircraft at Part 139 airports certificated for passenger traffic (Linnell et al. 1999, Cleary et al. 2005, Wright and Dolbeer 2005). Analyses of strike data from 2004-2008 indicated strike reporting at Part 139 airports had improved to 39 percent (Dolbeer 2009). Strike reporting for General Aviation (GA) aircraft is estimated at less than 5 percent (Dolbeer et al. 2008, Dolbeer 2009). Maximum values for reported losses are based on the assumption that the 20,216 reported strikes indicating an adverse effect represent, on average, 20 percent of the total strikes that occurred with commercial and GA aircraft from 1990–2012.

[3] Number of reports indicating 1 or more of the following: damage, negative effect on flight (EOF), downtime, repair costs, other costs.

Figures

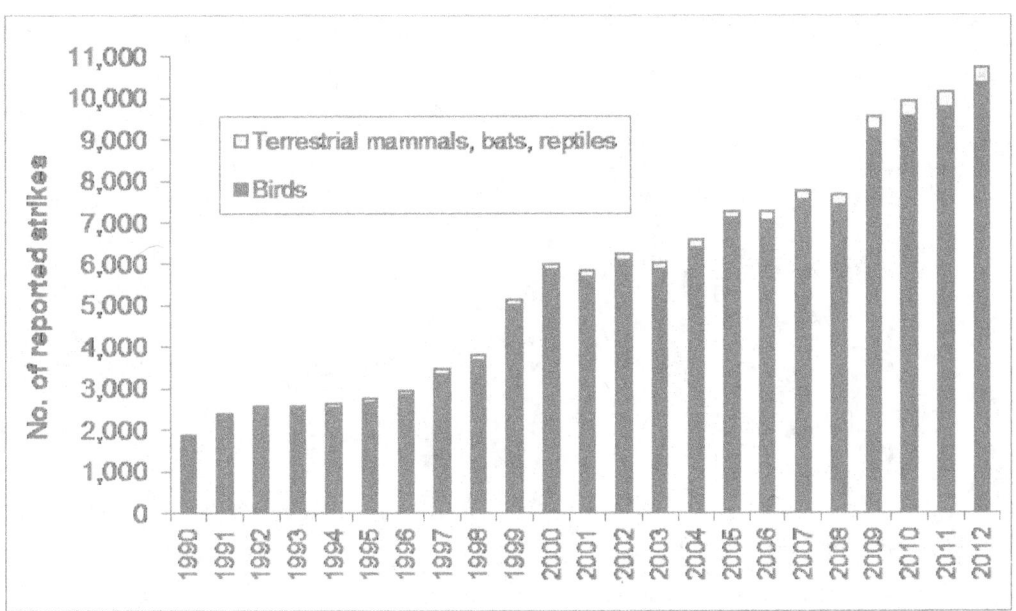

Figure 1. Number of reported wildlife strikes with civil aircraft, USA, 1990–2012. The 131,096 strikes involved birds (127,212), terrestrial mammals (2,946), bats (782), and reptiles (156, see Table 1).

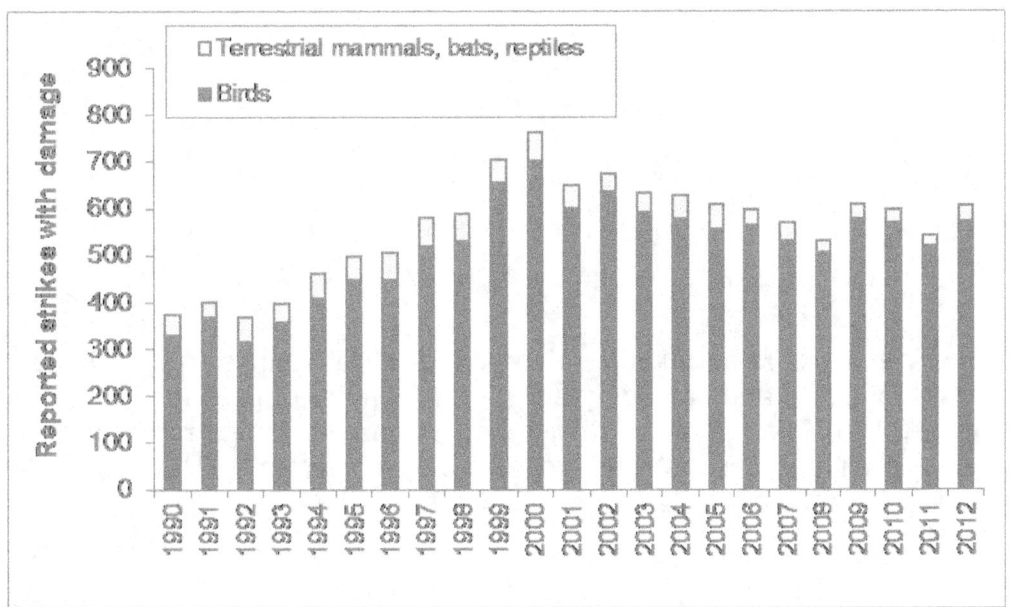

Figure 2. Number of reported wildlife strikes causing damage to civil aircraft, USA, 1990–2012. The 12,892 damaging strikes involved birds (11,883), terrestrial mammals (997), bats (10), and reptiles (2, see Table 1).

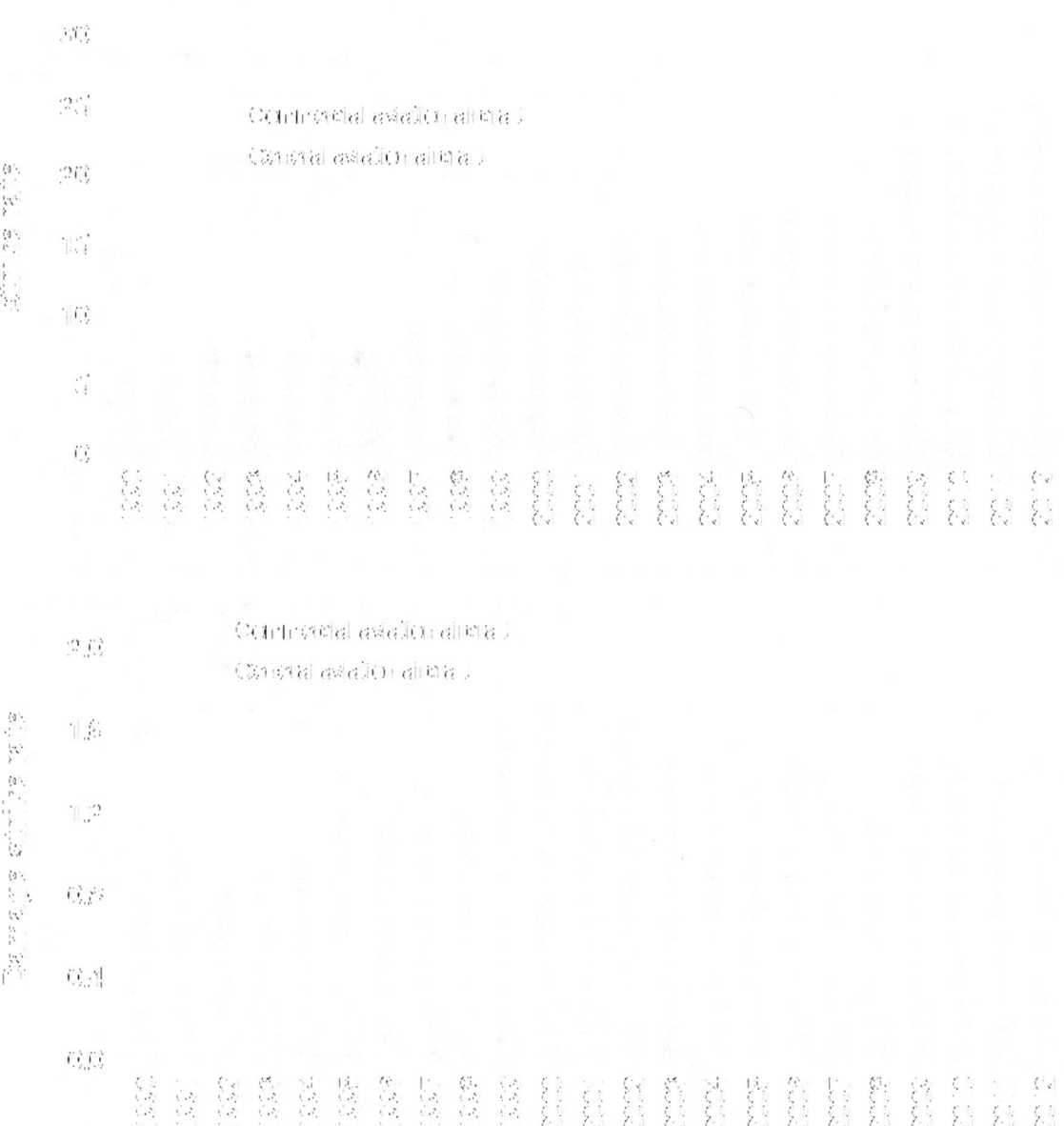

Figure 3. The strike rate (number of reported wildlife strikes per 100,000 aircraft movements, top graph) and damaging strike rate (number of reported damaging wildlife strikes per 100,000 aircraft movements, bottom graph) for commercial (air carrier, commuter, and air taxi service) and general aviation aircraft, USA, 1990–2012 (see Tables 2 and 3).

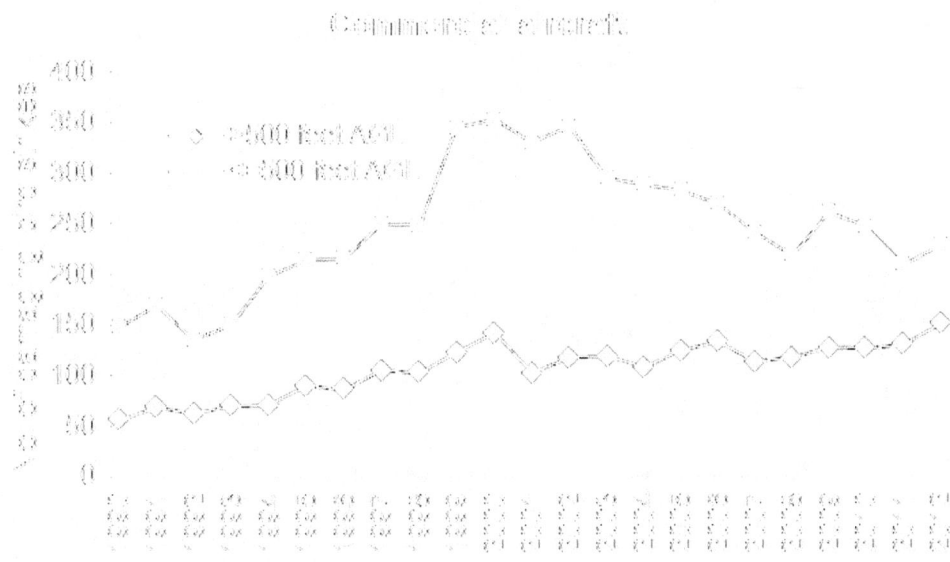

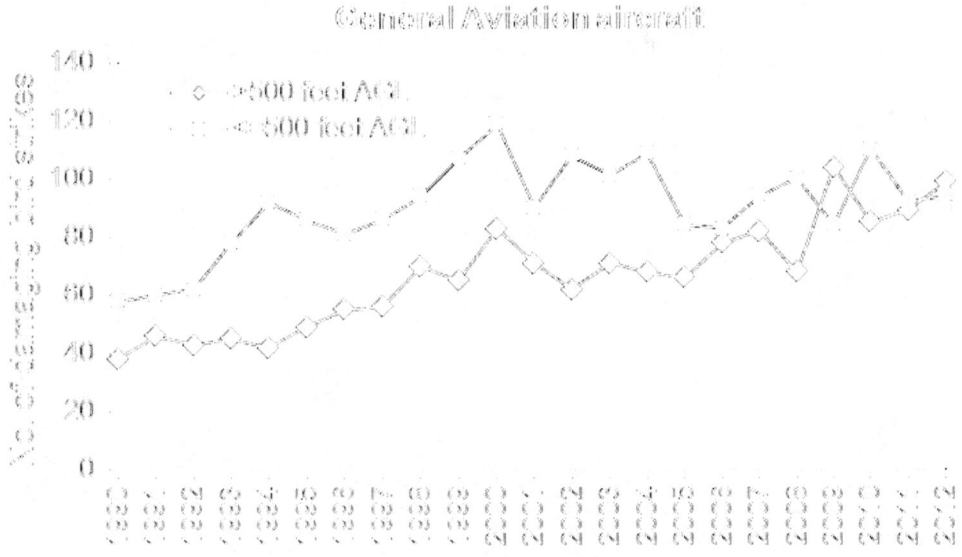

Figure 4. The number of damaging bird strikes with commercial (top graph) and general aviation (bottom graph) aircraft occurring at ≤ and >500 feet above ground level, USA, 1990–2012. Strikes with unknown height AGL reported are included in those at ≤500 feet AGL. See Tables 2 and 3 for sample sizes and Table 13 for classifications of damage.

Figure 5. Number of Part 139 certificated airports and General Aviation airports in USA with reported wildlife strikes and number of foreign airports at which strikes were reported for USA-registered civil aircraft, 1990–2012. Strikes were reported from 1,771 USA airports (531 Part 139 certificated, 1,240 General Aviation) and 273 foreign airports, 1990–2012 (Table 7).

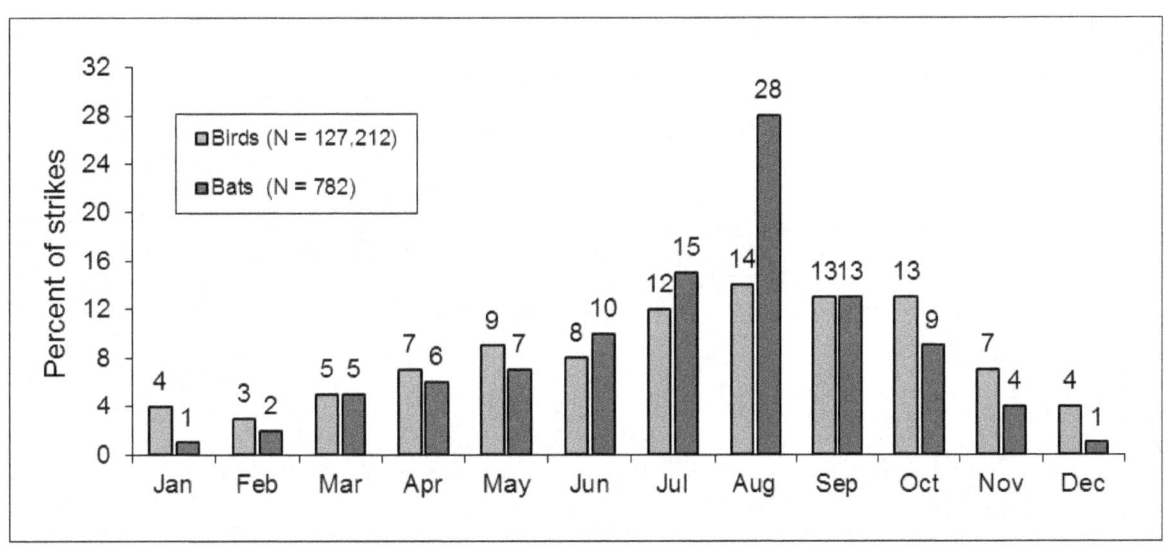

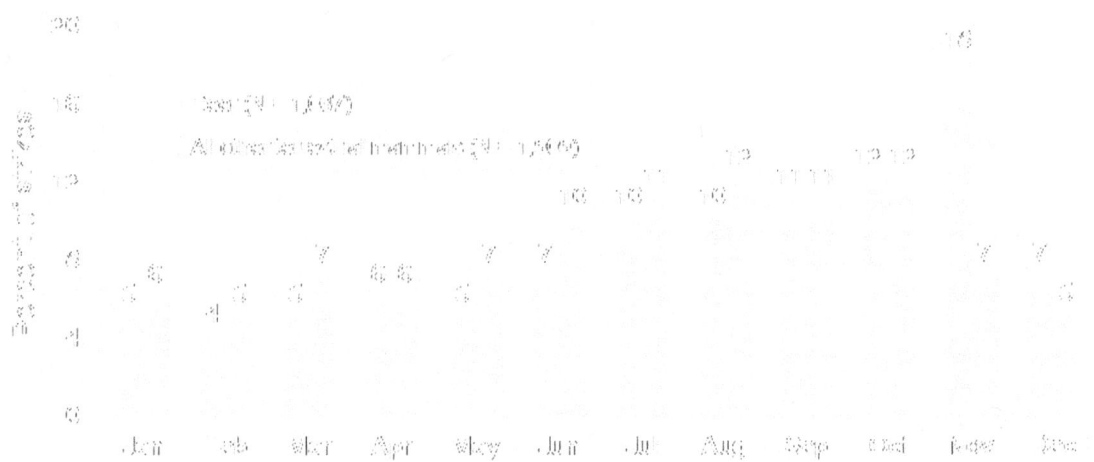

Figure 6. The percentage of reported bird and bat strikes (top graph) and deer and other terrestrial mammal strikes (bottom graph) with civil aircraft by month, USA, 1990–2012. In addition, 156 strikes with reptiles were reported of which 49 percent occurred in May–June. Deer strikes were comprised of 950 white-tailed deer, 65 mule deer, and 22 deer not identified to species. Biondi et al. (2011) provide a detailed analysis of deer strikes with civil aircraft in the USA.

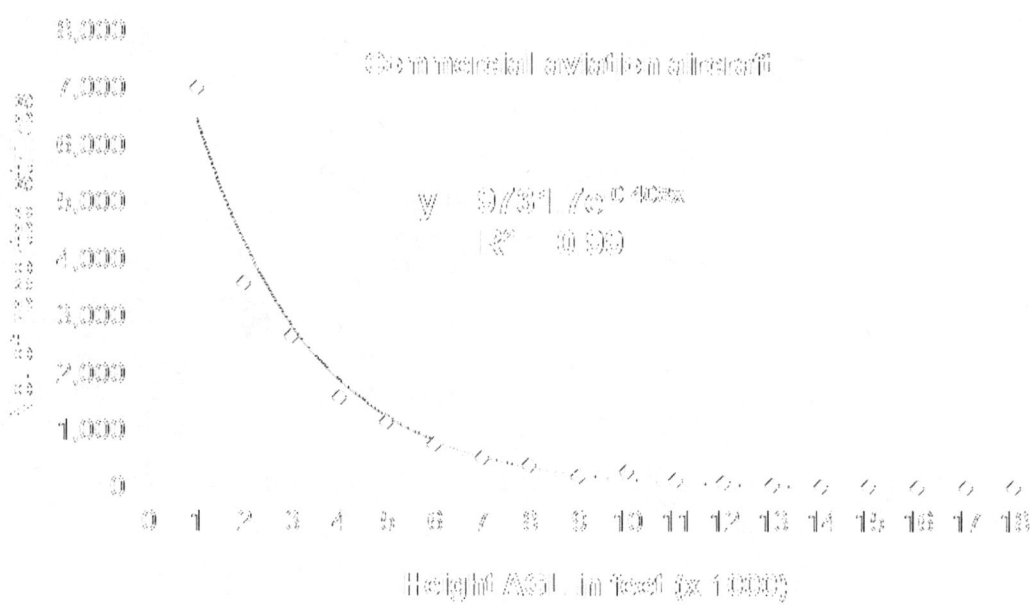

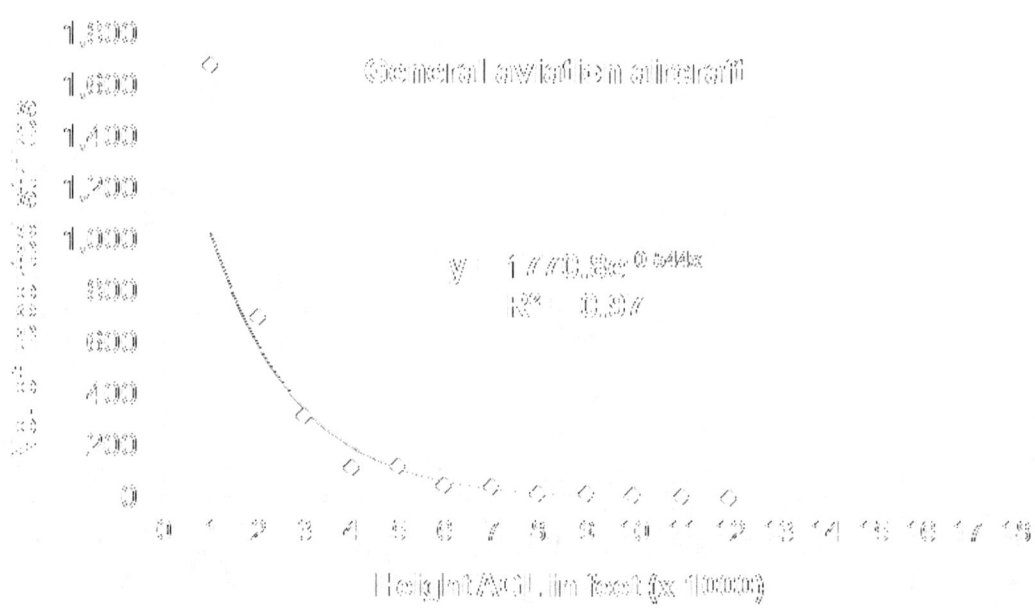

Figure 7. Number of reported bird strikes with commercial (top graph) and general aviation aircraft (bottom graph) in USA from 1990–2012 by 1,000-foot height intervals above ground level from 501–1,500 feet (interval 1) to 17,501–18,500 feet (interval 18). These graphs exclude strikes occurring at 500 feet or less. Above 500 feet, the number of reported strikes declined consistently by 34 percent and 42 percent for each 1,000 foot gain in height for commercial and general aviation aircraft, respectively. The negative exponential equations explained 97 to 99 percent of the variation in number of strikes by 1,000-foot intervals from 501 to 18,500 feet. See Tables 10 and 11 for sample sizes.

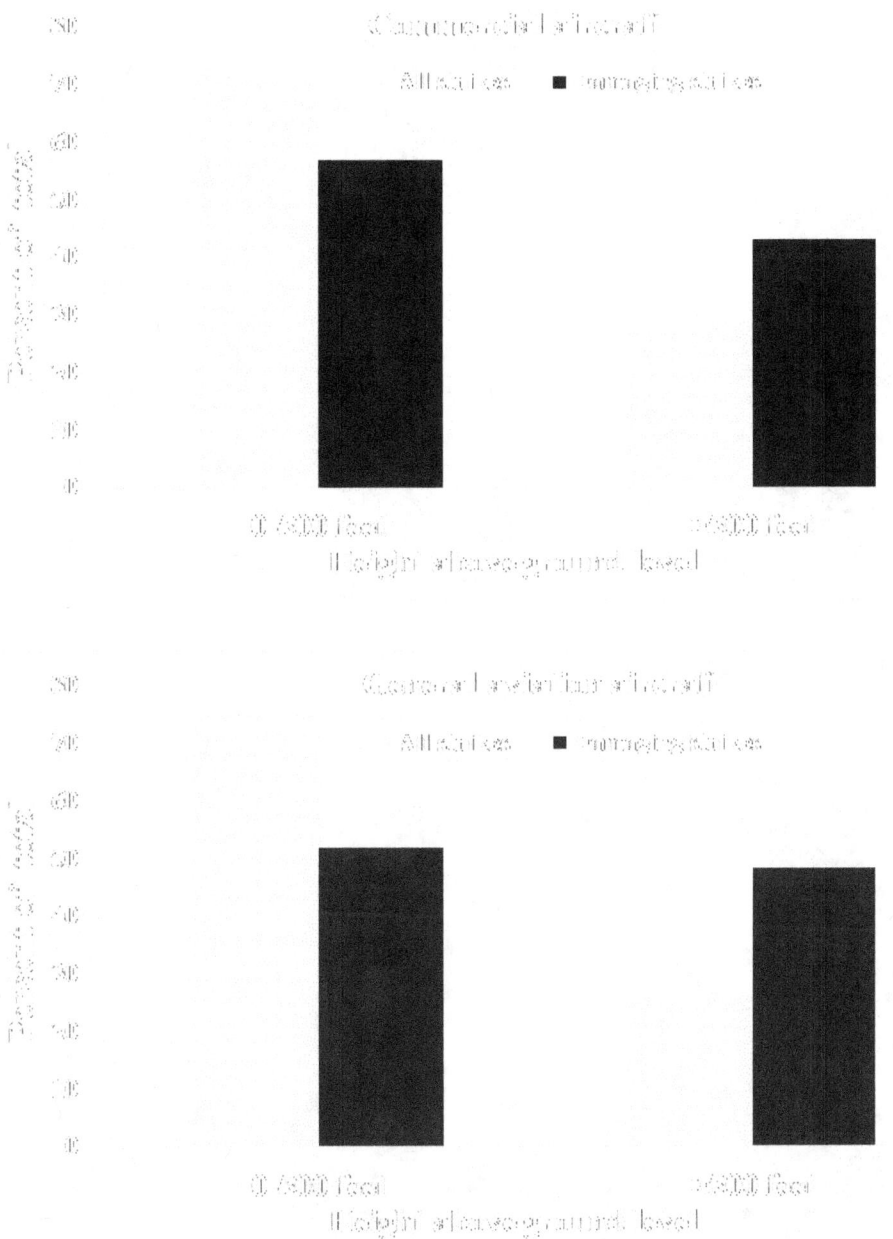

Figure 8. Percentage of total strikes and percentage of total damaging strikes occurring at 500 feet or less and above 500 feet for commercial (top graph) and general aviation (bottom graph) aircraft in USA, 1990–2012. See Tables 10 and 11 for sample sizes.

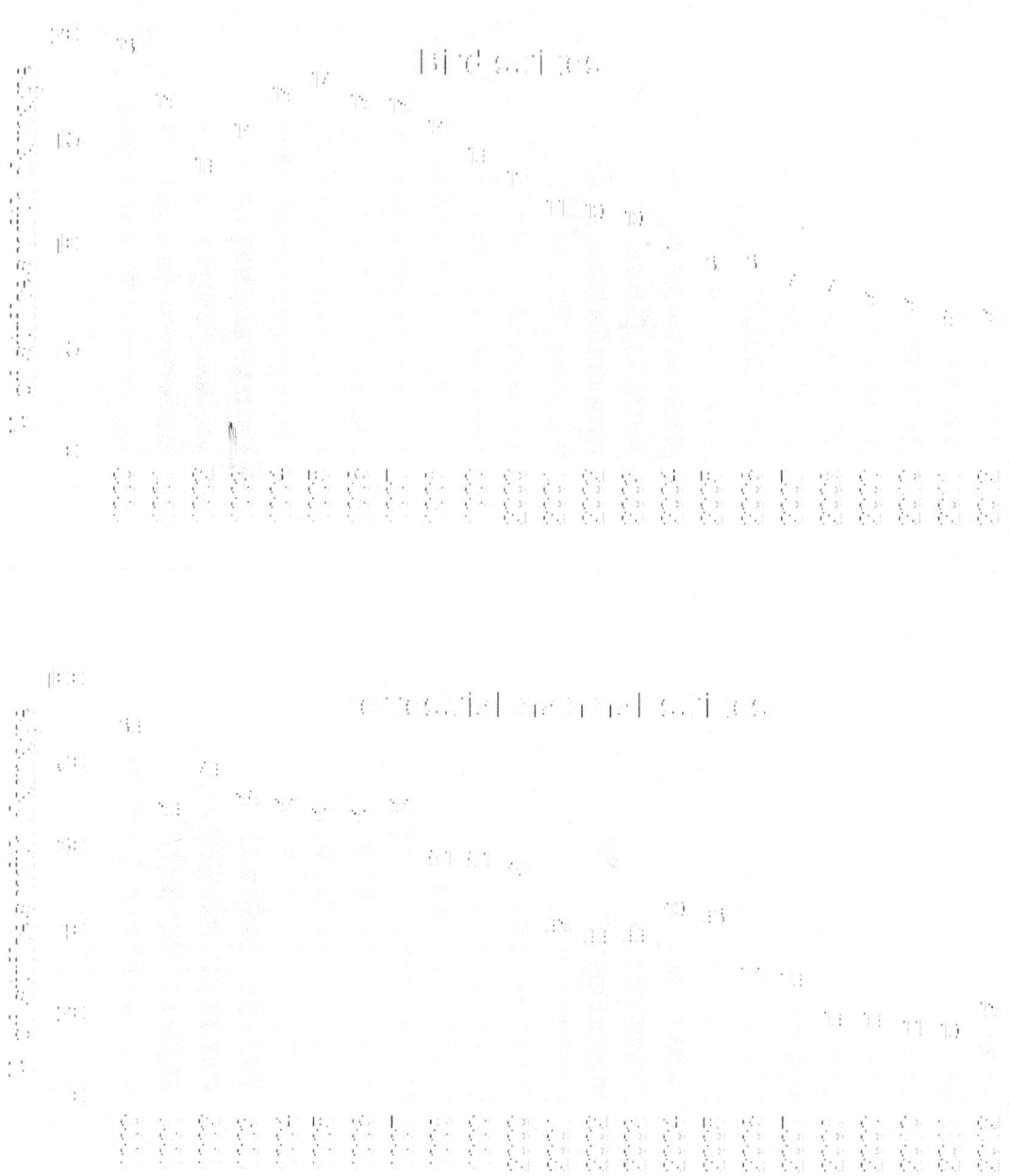

Figure 9. The percentage of reported bird strikes (top graph) and terrestrial mammal strikes (bottom graph) that indicated damage to the civil aircraft, USA, 1990–2012. See Tables 1 and 13 for sample sizes and classifications of damage.

Figure 10. Number of reported incidents where pilot made an emergency or precautionary landing after striking birds during departure in which fuel was jettisoned or burned (circling pattern) to lighten aircraft weight or in which an overweight (greater than maximum landing weight) landing was made (no fuel jettison or burn), USA civil aircraft, 1990–2012. See Table 15 for details on aircraft involved and amount of fuel jettisoned.

Figure 11. Number of reported incidents in which pilot made an aborted take-off at ≥80 knots after striking birds or other wildlife during take-off run, USA civil aircraft, 1990–2012. See Table 16 for classification of aborted take-offs by speed of aircraft.

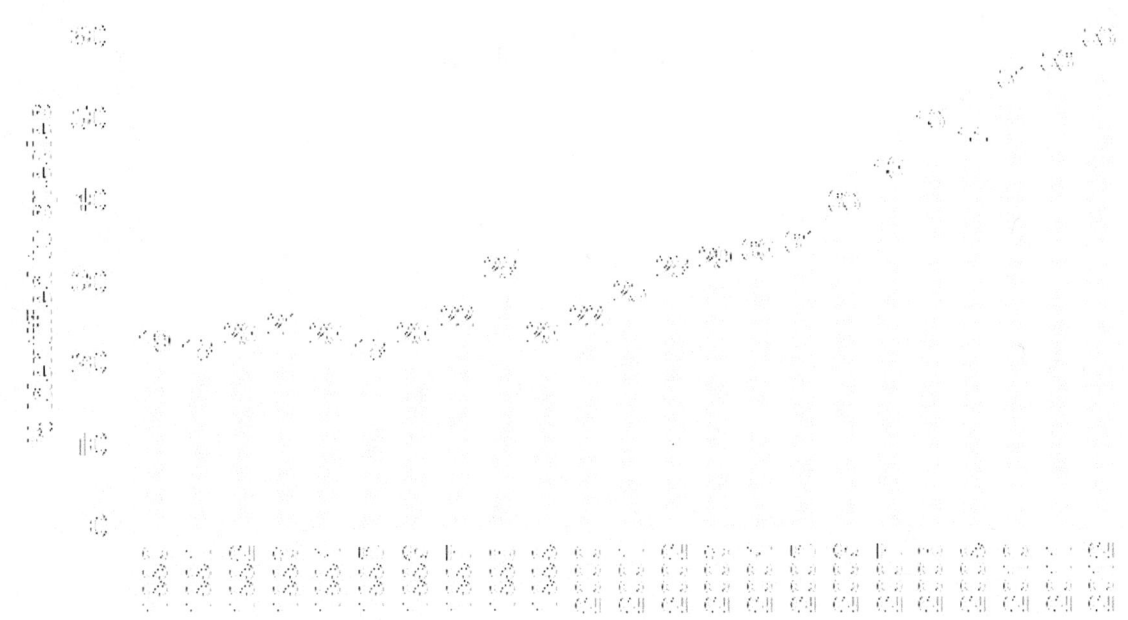

Figure 12. The percentage of reported bird strikes with civil aircraft in which the bird was identified to exact species, USA, 1990–2012. See Tables 1 and 17 for sample sizes.

This page intentionally left blank

APPENDIX A.
SELECTED SIGNIFICANT WILDLIFE STRIKES TO U.S. CIVIL AIRCRAFT, 2012

The U.S. Department of Agriculture, through an interagency agreement with the Federal Aviation Administration, compiles a database of all reported wildlife strikes to U.S. civil aircraft and to foreign carriers experiencing strikes in the USA. We compiled 127,212 strike reports from 1,771 USA airports and 273 foreign airports for 1990 through 2012 (10,726 strikes from 643 airports in 2012, Tables 1, 7; Figure 5). The following examples from the database in 2012 are presented to show the serious impact that strikes by birds or other wildlife can have on aircraft. These examples, from throughout the USA, demonstrate the widespread and diverse nature of the problem. The examples are not intended to highlight or criticize individual airports because, as documented above, strikes have occurred on almost every airport in the USA. Some of the strike examples reported here occurred off airport property during approach or departure. For more information on wildlife strikes or to report a strike, visit http://www.birdstrike.org and http://wildlife.faa.gov.

Date:	2 January 2012
Aircraft	BE-58
Airport:	Lambert-St Louis International (MO)
Phase of Flight:	Approach (3,900 feet AGL)
Effect on Flight:	Degraded performance
Damage:	Windshield, fuselage, tail
Wildlife Species:	Mallard or black duck
Comments from Report: Multiple bird strike caused two "almost basketball-size" holes in front windscreen, damaged rear left horizontal stabilizer and metal on top of fuselage. ID by Smithsonian, Division of Birds as either mallard or black ducks. Time out of service 5 days. Cost was $40,300.	

Date:	21 January 2012
Aircraft	B-737-800
Airport:	Sacramento International (CA)
Phase of Flight:	Climb (1,200 feet AGL)
Effect on Flight:	Precautionary landing, emergency declared
Damage:	Engines
Wildlife Species:	Greater white-fronted goose
Comments from Report: Two engines were damaged when geese were struck during climb out. The aircraft returned to land after declaring an emergency. Fan blades were damaged in both engines Passengers were rebooked on other flights. ID by Smithsonian, Division of Birds.	

Date:	17 February 2012
Aircraft	Eurocopter EC 130
Airport:	Near Paris, TN
Phase of Flight:	En Route (1,600 feet AGL)
Effect on Flight:	Landed in a field
Damage:	Windshield
Wildlife Species:	Mallard

Comments from Report: While en route to pick up a patient for transport, a duck broke through the right windscreen. The pilot maintained control and landed in a field. There were no injuries. The aircraft had to be trucked out for repairs. Time out of service was 3 days and costs estimated at $100,000.

Date:	1 March 2012
Aircraft	MD-11
Airport:	Memphis International (TN)
Phase of Flight:	Climb (8,500 feet AGL)
Effect on Flight:	Precautionary landing, emergency declared
Damage:	Radome, nose, engine, wing, fuselage
Wildlife Species:	Snow goose

Comments from Report: Preliminary information shows that 75% of the compressor blades were damaged. The engine cowling and radome were both heavily damaged. There is a hole in the leading edge of the left wing and side of fuselage forward of the right wing. The lower E & E compartment access door is damaged. There are numerous dents on the forward fuselage. At least 12 impact points were noted. ID by WS biologist. Costs totaled $2,739,462. Time out of service was 22 days.

Date:	6 March 2012
Aircraft	B-767-300
Airport:	Portland International (OR)
Phase of Flight:	Landing roll
Effect on Flight:	None
Damage:	Engine
Wildlife Species:	Canada goose

Comments from Report: Upon landing, while engines were in thrust reverse mode, a bird was ingested causing extensive damage to fan blades, acoustic shield and inlet. Engine was removed for repair. Pilot reported excess vibration and a strange noise. Runway was closed for 1.5 hours for clean up. Next flight was delayed 14 hours. Meal and transport vouchers were issued to passengers. ID by Smithsonian, Division of Birds. Costs estimated to be $378,000 and time out of service was 48 hours.

Date:	19 April 2012
Aircraft	B-757-200
Airport:	John F. Kennedy International (NY)
Phase of Flight:	Climb (800 feet AGL)
Effect on Flight:	Engine shut down, emergency landing
Damage:	Engine
Wildlife Species:	Double-crested cormorant
Comments from Report: Captain saw a flock of birds (15-20) during climb out. Birds were ingested into the #2 engine causing the captain to shut the engine down and return to land about 10 minutes later. The engine suffered extensive internal damage. Runway sweep found no remains, but a sample was taken from the engine for submission. ID by Smithsonian, Division of Birds. A passenger near the engine took a video of the birds.	

Date:	1 May 2012
Aircraft	C-172
Airport:	Three Rivers Municipal (MI)
Phase of Flight:	Climb (1 foot AGL)
Effect on Flight:	Emergency landing
Damage:	Propeller, nose, fuselage, wing strut, landing gear
Wildlife Species:	White-tailed deer
Comments from Report: Pilot was performing touch and go maneuvers when the aircraft hit a deer. Although the aircraft sustained substantial damage, the pilot was able to make a safe landing in Kalamazoo. The aircraft was sold for salvage.	

Date:	4 June 2012
Aircraft	Bell 427
Airport:	Near Indiantown, FL
Phase of Flight:	En Route (800 feet AGL)
Effect on Flight:	Emergency landing, hard landing
Damage:	Rotor head, pitch change rods
Wildlife Species:	Black vulture
Comments from Report: Pilot tried to avoid the birds but felt something impact the upper right side near the main rotor mast area. Pilot elected to land in an open field The aircraft went into a spin and hit the ground hard then rolled over on its side. Everyone on board was able to exit on their own. Five people received minor injuries. NTSB investigated. ID by Smithsonian, Division of Birds.	

Date:	14 June 2012
Aircraft	Embraer 175
Airport:	Minneapolis-St Paul International (MN)
Phase of Flight:	Climb (250 feet AGL)
Effect on Flight:	Engine shut down, precautionary landing
Damage:	Engine
Wildlife Species:	American coot
Comments from Report: During climb-out the engine ingested a bird or birds. Aircraft returned to land. The engine was totaled. Estimated cost was reported as $5 million for a new engine. ID by Smithsonian, Division of Birds.	

Date:	14 June 2012
Aircraft	C-560
Airport:	Lee C Fine Memorial (MO)
Phase of Flight:	Landing roll
Effect on Flight:	Unknown
Damage:	Landing gear
Wildlife Species:	White-tailed deer

Comments from Report: Aircraft struck a deer on landing. Bent nose wheel actuator. Ferried for repairs. Substantial damage. Time out of service was 75 days. Cost of repairs totaled $190,000.

Date:	6 July 2012
Aircraft	Grumman AA-5A
Airport:	Ray Community (MI)
Phase of Flight:	Approach (3 feet AGL)
Effect on Flight:	Avoidance maneuver
Damage:	Destroyed
Wildlife Species:	White-tailed deer

Comments from Report: Pilot saw two deer near the runway. One ran across the runway and the pilot tried to avoid it. The deer struck the left wing and the plane went into a field. The nose gear was sheared off and the engine cowling was crushed. The underside of the fuselage and right horizontal stabilizer were substantially damaged. The aircraft was destroyed. NTSB investigated.

Date:	9 July 2012
Aircraft	A-320
Airport:	Southwest Florida International (FL)
Phase of Flight:	Climb (2,000 feet AGL)
Effect on Flight:	Engine shut down, precautionary landing
Damage:	Engine
Wildlife Species:	Black vulture

Comments from Report: Engine ingestion caused compressor failure. Aircraft landed safely back at airport. Flight was cancelled. ID by Smithsonian, Division of Birds. Cost totaled $2 million. Aircraft was out of service 2 days.

Date:	31 July 2012
Aircraft	B-737-900
Airport:	Denver International (CO)
Phase of Flight:	Approach (5,500 feet AGL)
Effect on Flight:	Emergency landing
Damage:	Radome, nose, tail, pitot
Wildlife Species:	White-faced ibis

Comments from Report: Aircraft struck birds 25 miles east of airport. Flight was re-routed to the nearest runway due to loss of airspeed sensor and limited visibility. Captain's pitot was damaged. Nose cone had a large dent and nose had a 10" x 14" hole. Vertical stabilizer had a small dent. Feather remains found in engine but no engine damage. NTSB investigated. ID by Smithsonian, Division of Birds.

Date:	14 August 2012
Aircraft	EMB 170
Airport:	Charleston AFB International (SC)
Phase of Flight:	Climb (3,000 feet AGL)
Effect on Flight:	Precautionary landing
Damage:	Engine
Wildlife Species:	Anhinga

Comments from Report: Aircraft struck several birds about 2 miles east of the airport. The right hand engine ingested a number of birds causing fan blade and acoustic panel damage. The aircraft returned for a safe landing. Passengers were rebooked on other flights. Aircraft was out of service 42 hours. ID by Smithsonian, Division of Birds.

Date:	20 September 2012
Aircraft	Learjet 36
Airport:	Tweed-New Haven (CT)
Phase of Flight:	Take-off run
Effect on Flight:	Aborted take-off
Damage:	Wing, landing gear
Wildlife Species:	White-tailed deer

Comments from Report: Aircraft struck a deer on take-off roll at 100 knots. The pilot aborted take-off. Damage was found to the right wing near the fuselage and the right main landing gear. A patient was on board the air ambulance and was taken back to the hospital while the plane was being assessed. There were no injuries. Cost estimated to be in the millions.

Date:	2 October 2012
Aircraft	C-550
Airport:	Great Falls International (MT)
Phase of Flight:	Climb (100 feet AGL)
Effect on Flight:	Precautionary landing
Damage:	Engine
Wildlife Species:	Merlin

Comments from Report: The #1 engine fan section was damaged and the engine was replaced. ID by Smithsonian, Division of Birds. Cost was $500,000.

Date:	3 October 2012
Aircraft	B-737-300
Airport:	Bradley International (CT)
Phase of Flight:	Descent (15,000 feet AGL)
Effect on Flight:	Emergency landing
Damage:	Radome, fuselage
Wildlife Species:	Northern shoveler

Comments from Report: During descent over Long Island Sound at about 15,000 feet AGL a loud bang was heard followed by loud air noise. The aircraft was in heavy cloud cover and visibility was poor. No birds were seen. Pilot declared an emergency. Aircraft landed safely. The fuselage and radome had significant damage. Skin was torn back from structural areas. ID by Smithsonian, Division of Birds. Aircraft was out of service for almost 3 days.

Date:	25 October 2012
Aircraft	B-757-200
Airport:	Boise Air Terminal/Gowen Field (ID)
Phase of Flight:	Climb (12,000 feet AGL)
Effect on Flight:	Precautionary landing
Damage:	Radome, nose, engine
Wildlife Species:	Snow goose

Comments from Report: Two to ten snow geese were struck at 12,000 feet MSL during climb. A precautionary landing was made at departure airport. There was extensive damage to the radome and the #2 engine. Aircraft was out of service for 12 days. ID by Smithsonian, Division of Birds.

Date:	17 November 2012
Aircraft	Cessna 550
Airport:	Greenwood County (SC)
Phase of Flight:	Landing roll
Effect on Flight:	Other
Damage:	Aircraft destroyed
Wildlife Species:	White-tailed deer

Comments from Report: Aircraft struck a deer just after touchdown. The deer struck the left leading edge of the left wing above the left main landing gear and ruptured an adjacent fuel cell. The pilot maintained directional control and stopped on the runway spilling fuel and on fire. The plane ignited a brush fire. The aircraft was destroyed in the blaze. Pilot and passenger got out safely. There were no injuries.

Date:	21 November 2012
Aircraft	Cessna 402
Airport:	Over Atlantic Ocean near Barnstable, MA
Phase of Flight:	En Route (2000 feet AGL)
Effect on Flight:	Precautionary landing
Damage:	Windshield, interior
Wildlife Species:	Red-throated loon

Comments from Report: While en route from Barnstable to Nantucket over the ocean, a loon shattered the co-pilot's windshield. The aircraft, pilots and passengers were splattered with blood. The co-pilot was cut and later treated in the ER. The aircraft returned to Barnstable Municipal Airport for a safe landing. Time out of service was 1 week; cost of repairs was $15,000.

Date:	5 December 2012
Aircraft	CRJ 200
Airport:	La Guardia (NY)
Phase of Flight:	Approach (7,000 feet AGL)
Effect on Flight:	Other
Damage:	Radome, wing, fuselage
Wildlife Species:	Snow goose

Comments from Report: While on approach encountered multiple birdstrikes. Right wing leading edge, fuselage and radome were damaged. Emergency equipment escorted aircraft to the gate. ID by Smithsonian, Division of Birds. Time out of service was 38 days; costs totaled $370,678.

Date:	18 December 2012
Aircraft	Eurocopter AS 350
Airport:	Over the Florida Turnpike (FL)
Phase of Flight:	En Route (500 feet AGL)
Effect on Flight:	Precautionary landing
Damage:	Windshield
Wildlife Species:	Turkey vulture
Comments from Report: Miami-Dade Police Department helicopter made a precautionary landing at a Florida Turnpike Service Plaza following a birdstrike that broke the windshield and injured the pilot. Helicopter was removed on a flatbed truck.	

This page intentionally left blank

APPENDIX B. 2011– 2012 "REPORT WILDLIFE STRIKES" POSTER

This page intentionally left blank